LOVE IS FOR LIVING

LOVE IS FOR LIVING

by

CARLO CARRETTO

translated by

JEREMY MOISER

ORBIS BOOKS

Maryknoll, New York 10545

1977

Library of Congress Cataloging in Publication Data

Carretto, Carlo.
    Love is for living.

    Translation of Ciò che conta è amare.
    Reprint of the 1976 ed. published by Darton,
Longman and Todd, London.
    1.   Bible—Meditations.   I.   Title.
[BS483.5.C3413 1976]   242   76-49878
ISBN 0-88344-291-4

Originally published as Ciò che Conta è amare,
Editrice A.V.E., Rome

This translation copyright © Darton, Longman and Todd Ltd. 1976

All biblical quotations are from THE JERUSALEM BIBLE, Copyright © 1975
Darton, Longman and Todd Ltd. and Doubleday and Company, Inc.

Manufactured in the United States of America

CONTENTS

PART III

PART IV

FOREWORD

When I was about twenty, I had the great fortune to discover the Bible, and I have ever since set this down as one of the greatest moments of my life.

It was to this discovery, I am quite certain, that I owe that spark of spiritual fervour which led me first to an apostolate in the world and then to the contemplative life of the Little Brothers of Father de Foucauld.

The Bible has never let me down. It has given me everything I have needed, stage by stage. It has been with me as my faith has grown from the ardent enthusiasm of youth to the crucible of the desert, in which the soul, deprived of all external help and a prey to the most painful dryness, is twisted and shaken like a leaf in the storm of the Spirit. It is the only book I have always carried with me, and it is the book I wish my brothers to place on my breast with the crucifix and rosary when I am let down into the grave.

But before then – if I have time and if God my Lord wills it – I should like to read it over with those who do not know it, either because they have never bought it or because they have bought it but have been discouraged by the first difficulties. I should like to read it with the simple, the poor, with those who, like myself, have no formal exegetical training but who possess the one thing necessary: the desire to know the book of God.

I confess that this has always been my wish, and I have often dreamed of sitting beside someone and saying: let's start here, and then go on to there, and there, and there; and the pupil learns to walk alone on the path to his discovery of God's word.

Unfortunately little help comes to us from the past.

The Bible was almost a forbidden book. The Church experienced a dark age in which not even Christian families had a love for the Bible and the vast majority of Catholics had almost no knowledge of Scripture.

Happily things have changed, and the strong wind of the Spirit, which blew through the Church at Vatican II, is sweeping against the walls of ancient convents, battering the sacristies of a Christianity reduced to the miserable light of our own shortsightedness and shaking the laity who have remained ignorant of Christ because they were not allowed to read the Bible.

The terrible phrase is not mine, but I have experienced its truth like St Augustine its author: *Ignorantia Scipturarum ignorantia Christi* (He who has no knowledge of Scripture has no knowledge of Christ).

How true it is!

It is even truer in our own day, when so many Christians are forced to reconsider their position with regard to the faith. Taken off-guard by the recent rapid changes in the world, many find themselves asking: 'Do I still believe?' or 'Who is the God of my faith?' The reply is not always easy, especially for someone intent on demolishing the sentimental superstructures of his own religious past, the altars cluttered with saints but empty of sacrifices.

Even when a reply is given, the difficulties do not disappear.

There is widespread anxiety, particularly amongst those who felt they were free from unbelief and who in the past were convinced they had totally resolved the problem of God. 'Do I still believe?' And 'Who is the God of my faith?'

Yes, each of us has to ask himself in which God he believes: an unmysterious God, the product of his own wishful thinking and need for security, or the God of Abraham who leads us by paths not of our own choosing?

A miracle-working God who keeps us safe and comfortable, or the God of the crucified Jesus?

And if my God is the God of Abraham and the God of Jesus, where have I learnt to look for Him, to know Him, and to love Him?

Have I been satisfied with substitutes, or have I consulted the *real* book, the inspired book, the book which tells me what He is like, what He thinks and says and does? That book is the Bible, God's authentic word.

This is the truth which is daily gaining ground, the conviction Christians are acquiring under the guidance of the Spirit.

I am convinced that because of it we shall enjoy a glorious post-conciliar spring, a feature of which will be the return of Christians to the Bible.

The movement is irreversible, like the liturgical movement, like the rediscovery of love as the soul and fulness of the Christian message to the world.

Assured of the truth of this, I have tried in prayer to walk the paths where the divine wind is most felt. I have tried – if I may change the image – to collect in my little bowl as much of this saving grace raining down on the Church as I can.

How I long to describe God's action in souls, pitiful though my pen is!

How I should like to help even one young person who felt lost in his or her search for the God of Abraham, the God of Jesus. I should say to that young person: Trust the Book that God wrote for our instruction. Take the Bible, put it on your desk, say to yourself, 'From now on I shall make this book my very own; I shall keep it beside me, I shall never stop reading it, I shall try and understand everything God tells me.'

This in fact is the incalculable and irreplaceable value of the Bible: it is God who speaks, it is God who reveals Himself to the soul when the soul in humility and openness scans its pages for God's eternal will.

We must add one last word on the plan of the present work, which might well seem strange to some readers.

Writing a book is extremely simple: all one has to do is put one word after another. The difficulty is to get the book read: times are unsuitable.

It is not that most people are distracted or that Welfare State citizens prefer to look at the television or go to a concert.

The simple fact is that we bore people, we cannot present the things of God satisfyingly.

That is the real reason, and I admit I have no solution.

In the present case, dealing with the Bible, I should have been systematic, profound. But I had a shock. I discovered I was not a theologian, or a philosopher, or an exegete, I was nothing at all, and I should undoubtedly have given up the idea if I had not seen one good trump in my hand: the experience of a life of faith, *my* life of faith. So I thought I would start from there and offer the reader, in the form of daily meditations, what the Bible has told me in faith and continues to tell me in life.

The men of today believe in the value of existence, in the testimony of life, partly because, sometimes without knowing it, they look to the existential experience of others for a reflection of their own. In this they are not mistaken, and the proof is the Bible itself.

The Bible relates the history of God's People on their pilgrimage to the Promised Land. This journey is surely the exemplar of all the journeys of all men. In recounting our own history, we recount that of others: 'There is nothing new under the sun' (Qo 1:9).

But sometimes, reading human history, we conceive a wish to discover what makes it all tick, what lies behind the veil of our existence.

Then is the moment to go in search of it, to leave the guidance of human books behind and commit oneself totally to God's Book.

That is all there is to it.

The following biblical meditations are intended to be like the self-starter in a car. When the reader has come to an end of them, he will have only to engage the right gear, let the clutch in and set off on his journey of discovery into the Bible.

May the Spirit of the Lord give you and me the grace to feel the sweetness of His presence.

CARLO CARRETTO

INTRODUCTION

I wrote *Letters from the Desert** sitting on the arid dunes of the Sahara. They cost me ten years of suffering, and I love them for that. I tried to place myself, naked, poor and alone, in the presence of God's eternal Majesty, totally committed to penetrating the logic of the Gospels, which is inexhaustible. I tried to imagine myself in mind and heart beyond time, to visualize the Last Day, when He the Supreme Judge will come to separate the chaff from the wheat. I felt I was chaff. I could not deceive myself: I did not know what it meant to love.

In the face of Love's judgement I felt enclosed in my own infinite and omnipotent egoism, a freshly-cut log still full of sap, refusing to burn, merely smoking and sizzling.

This was why.

One evening, in the desert, I had met an old man shivering with cold. It might seem odd to call the desert cold, but cold it is: the Sahara has been defined as 'a cold country which is extremely hot when the sun shines'.

Anyway, the sun had set, and the old man was shivering.

I had two blankets with me – indispensable for warmth on a night in the open. Giving him one meant going cold myself.

I was afraid, and I kept both blankets for myself.

I did not shiver with the cold that night, but I trembled before God's judgement on the following day.

* London and Maryknoll, New York 1972.

I dreamt I had been killed in an accident, crushed by the weight under which I had gone to sleep.

With my body trapped under tons of granite but still alive – very much so! – I was judged.

The two blankets, nothing else, were the subject of the judgement.

I was declared unfit for the Kingdom, and I could see why.

I who had denied my brother a blanket for fear of the cold had failed to observe the commandment of God: 'You shall love your neighbour as yourself' (Lv 19:18). I had set greater store by my own skin than by his.

And there was more: I who, having accepted to imitate Jesus in becoming a Little Brother, had received the revelation of Christ, who loved His neighbour not only *as Himself* but, infinitely more, *to death on the cross*, had failed to observe my duty as His disciple.

How could I enter the Kingdom of Love in these conditions? I was rightly judged unfit and requested to remain outside until I had mended my ways. That was how my purgatory began.

In meditation and suffering I had to undergo the two stages of man's religious life on earth: the Old and the New Testaments, the former to convince to me of the truth of the first commandment, 'You shall love your neighbour as yourself', and the latter to impress on me the force of Jesus's words, 'Just as I have loved you, you also must love one another' (Jn 13:34), to the ultimate sacrifice.

In short, I had to learn to give both blankets, the first to show that I loved the old man as myself, the second to prove that, in imitation of Jesus, I was able to carry the sorrows of others.

Stripped of my blankets, shivering with the cold while my brother went warm, I should have entered the Kingdom of Love. But not until then!

I must confess that I was not prepared to do this, I was unfit. I had to start again from scratch, retrace the entire path, trying to understand Jesus's lesson better, trying to see the essence and not just the details of the Law, its spirit, not its letter.

But doing the journey again is no easy matter when one is old and tired and the road long, rough and difficult.

It is so much easier to stay put, or better still to die and so avoid all need to set out. 'Lord, I have had enough. Take my life; I am no better than my ancestors' (1 K 19:4), said Elijah sitting down under a furze bush.

The realization that we are as weak as others, 'no better than our ancestors', is such a shock to our pride that we prefer to die than attempt the difficult path of renewal.

But it is also the discovery of our true poverty, and this, ultimately, is a good and precious thing.

Once we realize we are poor, weak and empty, we can start again and give our lives a new direction.

This is precisely what Elijah did. Strengthened not by his own efforts but by the food left by God's angel, he 'walked for forty days and forty nights until he reached Horeb, the mountain of God' (1 K 19:8).

How I too should like to reach the mountain of God! That is now my only aspiration, my only dream: the mountain of God, the Horeb of contemplation, inner joy, deep endless peace, infinite love.

When I was a novice in the Sahara, the novice-master would occasionally invite us to undertake a period of 'real desert life'. With some bread, a few dates and the Bible in our knapsacks, we left for one of the many caves hollowed out from time immemorial in the spurs of the mountain. We had to live alone with God as far as possible, accepting the suffering of loneliness, the nausea of putting up with one's own company, the effort of arid and often painful prayer.

We had only one book with us, the Bible, because it is the only book worthy to stand open when God is present in naked faith and the soul struggles with him as Jacob struggled at Peniel (Gn 32:23–33).

14

I should like to set out once more in the same way, with no more than the Bible and some bread in my knapsack. I shall look for solitude for forty days, and I shall travel alone. I shall go beyond time, but without trying to escape that dreadful judgement of Love when I had refused the poor man my blankets: the lesson had to stay with me. It is in any case a journey I shall have to make sooner or later, and it is better to start it now, because *love is for living*.

PART I

If, like Elijah, we wish to cross the desert in search of God's revelation, we cannot afford to wander aimlessly. We have to follow a well-trodden path and commit ourselves with all the strength of nature and grace.

Faith, hope and charity are the shortest and safest path.

Our first seven meditations will be devoted to them.

Chapter One

IMMERSED IN THE LIGHT

> Half way on my journey through life
> I found myself in a dark wood
> Far from the path.

This is how Dante described himself at the age of thirty-five.

Alas, I did not wait so long to enter the dark wood of sin. I was there long before the poet, when I was only eighteen.

But then half way through life I was bathed in God's light, a full searching light which penetrated every corner of my being and filtered through it like sun through the leaves of a forest.

I feel immersed in God like a drop in the ocean, like a star in the immensity of night; like a lark in the summer sun or a fish in the sea.

More: in God I feel like a child in its mother's lap, and my finite freedom everywhere touches His Being which wraps me round tenderly; my need to grow and expand and my thirst for fulfilment are sated every minute by His living Presence.

I can do nothing without Him, I can see nothing except through Him.

There is no creature, thing, thought or idea which does not speak to me of Him and which is not a message from Him. 'Up, up to the outermost point of the universe and down, down to the utter limits of my own nothingness, I see Him.'

The entire universe is a Sacred Host which contains Him, speaks to me of Him and in which I adore Him as both immanent and transcendent, the root of my being, my beginning, support and final end: as *He Who Is*.

God is the sea in which I swim, the atmosphere in which I breathe, the reality in which I move.

I cannot find the tiniest thing which does not speak to me of Him, which is not somehow His image, His message, His call, His smile, His reproach, His word.

> The heavens declare the glory of God,
> the vault of heaven proclaims his handiwork;
> day discourses of it to day,
> night to night hands on the message.
>
> No utterance at all, no speech,
> no sound that anyone can hear;
> yet their voice goes out through all the earth,
> and their message to the ends of the world.
>
> (Ps 19:1-4)

And I feel like singing:

> Bless Yahweh, my soul.
> Yahweh my God, how great you are!
> Clothed in majesty and glory,
> wrapped in a robe of light!
>
> You stretch the heavens out like a tent,
> you build your palace on the waters above;
> using the clouds as your chariot,
> you advance on the wings of the wind;
> you use the winds as messengers
> and fiery flames as servants.
>
> (Ps 104:1-4)

I close my eyes and see God who 'shakes the earth':

> The sun, at his command, forbears to rise,
> and on the stars he sets a seal.

He and no other stretched out the skies,
    and trampled on the Sea's tall waves.
The Bear, Orion too, are of his making,
    the Pleiades and the Mansions of the South.
His works are great, beyond all reckoning,
    his marvels, beyond all counting.
Were he to pass me, I should not see him,
    nor detect his stealthy movement.
Were he to snatch a prize, who could prevent him,
    or dare to say, 'What are you doing?'

                                    (Jb 9:7–12)

How I tremble to talk with Him! I think the world must leap
at the sound of his voice. As I contemplate His greatness, I
think to myself:

Who was it measured the water of the sea in the
                                    hollow of his hand
and calculated the dimensions of the heavens,
gauged the whole earth to the bushel,
weighed the mountains in scales,
the hills in a balance?

Who could have advised the spirit of Yahweh,
what counsellor could have instructed him?
Whom has he consulted to enlighten him,
and to learn the path of justice
and discover the most skilful ways?

                                    (Is 40:12–14)

Everything disappears in comparison with the eternal God,
and the greatest things become as nothing:

See, the nations are like a drop on the pail's rim,
they count as a grain of dust on the scales.
See, the islands weigh no more than fine powder.

All the nations are as nothing in his presence,
for him they count as nothingness and emptiness.

(Is 40:15, 17)

Man's littleness is terrifying; and yet since the moment love bridged the gap I desire nothing more than to feel how small I am.

I am Yahweh, unrivalled;
there is no other God besides me.
Though you do not know me, I arm you
that men may know from the rising to the setting
of the sun
that apart from me all is nothing.
I am Yahweh, unrivalled,
I form the light and create the dark.
I make good fortune and create calamity,
it is I, Yahweh, who do all this.

(Is 45:5–7)

How odd doubt looks in these moments of light! How could I ever doubt God?

Can it argue with the man who fashioned it,
one vessel among earthen vessels?
Does the clay say to its fashioner, 'What are you
making?'
Woe to him who says to a father, 'What have you
begotten?'
or to a woman, 'To what have you given birth?'

(Is 45:9–10)

And such greatness is so close to us! Not only close, but in us, around us, because in Him 'we live, and move, and exist' (Ac 17:28).

22

For your great strength is always at your call;
who can withstand the might of your arm?
In your sight the whole world is like a grain of
                                    dust that tips the scales,
like a drop of morning dew falling on the ground.
Yet you are merciful to all, because you can do all
                                                        things
and overlook men's sins so that they can repent.
Yes, you love all that exists, you hold nothing of
                        what you have made in abhorrence,
for had you hated anything, you would not have
                                                    formed it.
And how, had you not willed it, could a thing
                                                    persist,
how be conserved if not called forth by you?
You spare all things because all things are yours,
                                    Lord, lover of life,
you whose imperishable spirit is in all.

                                        (Ws 11:21–6)

So much light!

And how easy it is to witness to the light! It is the priestly
function of man as man. Upright on earth, I feel that the
creatures turn to me so that I can voice their silent adoration of
God.

The wind, the fire, the dew and the frost, the ice and the
snow, the mountains and the hills, the springs and the seas
press on me from all sides. They seem to say: You must not fail
in your vocation to speak for us all in the sight of God.

And I pray:

> All things the Lord has made, bless the Lord:
> give glory and eternal praise to him.
> Heavens! bless the Lord:
> give glory and eternal praise to him.
> Sun and moon! bless the Lord:

give glory and eternal praise to him.
Showers and dews! all bless the Lord:
give glory and eternal praise to him.

(Dn 3:57, 59, 62, 64)

The more I sing God's praises, the more I feel that creatures thank me for having helped them express themselves and that they smile in happiness at my kingship.

I know that by adoring God I am performing a fundamental, eternal act, an act which is an end in itself and part and parcel of my being. It brings me happiness, total, lasting happiness. Nothing is left now but my promise for tomorrow:

I will remind you of the works of the Lord,
    and tell of what I have seen.
By the words of the Lord his works come into being
    and all creation obeys his will.
As the sun in shining looks on all things,
    so the work of the Lord is full of his glory.
He has fathomed the deep and the heart,
    and seen into their devious ways;
for the Most High knows all the knowledge there is,
    and has observed the signs of the times.
He declares what is past and what will be,
    and uncovers the traces of hidden things.
Not a thought escapes him,
    not a single word is hidden from him.
He has imposed an order on the magnificent
                                works of his wisdom,
    he is from everlasting to everlasting,
nothing can be added to him, nothing taken away,
    he needs no one's advice.
How desirable are all his works,
    how dazzling to the eye!
Who could ever be sated with gazing at his glory?

(Si 42:15–16, 18–22, 26b)

Chapter Two

FAITH

It is odd, but none the less true, that too much light can seem like darkness.

If I try and look at the sun, everything goes black.

Nothing could be truer, nothing more opaque, than the existence of God. Nothing could be clearer, more rational, more tangible than the creation of the universe by God, nothing more mysterious. Nothing could be more evident than the eternity of the soul, nothing more painfully dark at the moment of death.

In our relationship with the transcendent God we enter the regions of faith, and faith is dark, obscure, naked and often painful.

Whether we like it or not that is how the matter stands, and as we progress we see it must be so.

'At present we are looking at a confused reflection in a mirror', says St Paul (1 Co 13:12), and no amount of reasoning, however acute, can change that.

Because he is a creature, man is immersed in darkness, in the 'mystery' which is not a lack of light but the reflection of a light which far exceeds him. That light is so 'new' that he is obliged to undergo a gradual education and revelation which will engage his entire existence.

God could add nothing to what He has already done – and does – to explain things better, to make our relationship with Him easier, to convince us more of His existence and Providence.

What could He add to the immensity of the universe to express His own infinity? What would He achieve by making even more splendid the splendour of nature's beauty, or by improving the already staggering perfection of our nervous system and the laws which govern the universe?

Nothing at all.

The beauty, greatness and perfection in which we are immersed cannot exempt us from the act of faith, they cannot substitute for it.

Immersed in the light, we have to cry out, 'I believe in the light'; moved by the perfection of creation, we have to proclaim, 'I believe in Perfection'.

But that is not enough.

The gap between believing in a God who is immanent in His creation, in a God who is, as it were, visible to the naked eye, and believing in a God who transcends His creation is so great that we are forced to accept, in faith, that the transcendent God is unknown, that He is darkness to our human eyes.

He is and will always be – even in Heaven, when we shall see Him 'face to face', as Scripture says – the great Mystery.

However, this God has willed and wills to reveal Himself to man, to make Himself known: life on earth is given to us for this purpose, so is purgatory, so is Heaven. God discloses himself to man in time and in eternity, and this loving gift of Himself to us in the knowledge we can have of Him and in the love with which we shall possess Him will never come to an end. But there will always be something of His *Mystery*, and we shall never tire of contemplating it, of nourishing ourselves on His gradual revelation, of plunging into the sea of His hidden love and luxuriating in the possession of it.

The path and the hour of this knowledge both begin here on earth, firstly in the symbols and signs of creation, then in the lines and veils of Scripture, then in the existential experience of ourselves and the whole world, and finally in the contemplation and transforming union of the mystical life.

All of it takes place under the guidance of faith.

Seen in this context, faith is the certainty and guarantee of this gradual divine revelation; it is the bandage protecting man's sick, immature eyes from the pain of too much light; it is the patient teacher of the infant soul learning to walk without support; it is the instrument of God who knows all and who respects the gradual, logical development of man who knows nothing.

It is the testimony God gives us in Christ to the 'things that are above'; there is no testimony other than this.

Has anyone ever thought of communicating with the transcendence of God by human means? Has anyone ever thought there could be a voice or presence clarifying the Mystery without the need for faith? Yes. Jesus Himself tells us in the parable of Dives and Lazarus (Lk 16:19–31).

For denying the poor man the scraps from his table, the rich man, who 'used to dress in purple and fine linen and feast magnificently every day', went to hell when he died and was there tormented.

In his agony he bethought himself of his five brothers at home and begged Abraham 'to send Lazarus to his father's house to give them warning so that they did not come to this place of torment too'.

Abraham replied that it would serve no purpose: 'They have Moses and the prophets, let them listen to them.'

The rich man insisted: 'They will repent', he said, 'if someone comes to them from the dead.'

'If they will not listen to Moses or to the prophets', retorted Abraham, 'they will not be convinced even if someone should rise from the dead.'

How many times, especially in our younger days, have we thought like the rich man? 'If someone comes from the dead' – no, says Jesus, it would be useless, 'you would not be convinced even if someone should rise from the dead.'

Just imagine what would happen if Lazarus came down

from Abraham's bosom and addressed you from beyond the grave. Imagine he came to you one night, while you were lying alone in bed. Imagine his talking to you, telling you what you should do, etc.

Even before dawn, once you had recovered from your surprise, you would probably be saying to yourselves: 'I had indigestion last night. It gave me bad dreams.'

And after a good breakfast you would carry on living just as before, no better, no worse. And so should I. It would be Father Malachy's miracle all over again.

No, there is no human substitute for *faith*. We cannot avoid *believing*. There is no way round the enormous effort of 'living by faith', not even miracles.

Crowds witnessed the multiplication of the loaves by the lake and 'had enough to eat', but few believed in Jesus, and at the first difficulty in the so-called Discourse on the Bread of Life (Jn 6:32–66) many of His disciples 'left him and stopped going with him'.

Crowds saw the resurrection of Lazarus (Jn 11), but few believed in the Man who had done it. Some even decided to do away with Him because He was an obstacle to their plans.

No, not even miracles exempt us from living by faith, from walking in the faith. They can do no more than help us by witnessing.

Is this assistance rare? Surely it fills the space surrounding us? Is there any creature which does not speak to us of *Him*? which is not His photograph and symbol? which is not an invitation from Him?

Are we not immersed in the sublime, in the immense, in the beautiful, in the perfect, dreaming the most extraordinary dream? Are we not part of an infinite multiplicity continually being reduced to the most fantastic unity? If we look through creation, do we not see *God*?

Is not the immensity of the universe an image of *His* immensity?

Is not He, and only He, the reply to all our questions?

Yes, He is, most definitely!

The problem, however, remains: our relationship or dialogue with God, our discovery of God, takes place in faith and only in faith.

Chapter Three

THE CALL TO FAITH

The paradigm of every call to faith, the most impressive model of every human story about faith, the most stirring pages of man's epic struggle in his dialogue with God are contained in chapters 12 to 25 of the Book of Genesis.

It is the story of Abraham.

Yahweh said to Abraham, 'Leave your country, your family and your father's house, for the land I will show you. I will make you a great nation; I will bless you and make your name so famous that it will be used as a blessing.

I will bless those who bless you:
I will curse those who slight you.
All the tribes of the earth
shall bless themselves by you.'

(Gn 12:1–3)

This is the mystery of God's 'call', the mystery of our 'vocation'.

It takes place in the darkness of faith, and all human reasoning is powerless to penetrate it.

How did Abraham 'pick up' the divine message? How did John XXIII hear at fourteen the voice which told him he would be a priest? How did each one of us find his path in life?

The answer is: by faith, and that is a new dimension at work in us, one which does not start from reason, one which, while not contradicting reason, surpasses it infinitely because it can reach God: in faith, the soul is invited to establish a living relationship with God, to see Him, listen to Him and speak with Him.

Abraham is the ancestral head of all men of faith, of all those whose lives enjoy this new dimension, who accept the risks and the consequences. He is the founder of the family of believers, he stands at the head of the 'people of God', those mysterious folk who puncture reality and carry on beyond things, who hear the voices coming from the other side, who travel beyond time into eternity, looking for the Absolute, the Infinite, who consider themselves to be exiles on earth, perpetual nomads, who are not satisfied with what they can see but look for the invisible God, who learn to find Him everywhere and who obey Him as a King, as a Tremendous Lover.

In short, Abraham is the model of those who respond to God's call.

That call never ceases: God is always calling, but there are special moments which we record in our memories or perhaps in a note-book and which we never forget.

Abraham did not forget that first summons: 'Leave your country, your family and your father's house, for the land I will show you.' Abram (as he then was) left his country and followed the voice.

Abram was seventy-five years old when he left Haran. He took his wife Sarai, his nephew Lot, all the possessions they had amassed and the people they had acquired in Haran. They set off for the land of Canaan.

(Gn 12:4–5)

Man's vocation or call is a moment of light, an unexpected gleam in the darkness, a gap in the fog, a star among the clouds, a lighthouse in a storm at sea.

Once the call has sounded, there is no doubt as to which way to go. Some people worry about how the Lord spoke to Abram or St Francis. Such worry is useless as we shall

31

never know. God appears to each individual in the most suitable way to make him understand what is wanted of him, and God is not short of means. To Mary He sent an angel; to Joseph He spoke in a dream, to Moses in a burning bush, to Elijah in the sound of a gentle breeze.

The important thing is that God speaks and the soul listens and understands.

If God did not speak, what other voice could ever reach into our frightful solitude? If God did not call, who would ever rescue us from our nothingness? Our faith rests on the certainty that God is looking for us, that He breaks through our isolation to lead us where He wills, to create our happiness, bring us to our final end, quench our thirst for ever.

Abraham's vocation took place in three stages: a call to detachment; an eternal promise; a severe test.

We have already mentioned the first of these. Abram was asked to leave his country, his people, his paternal roof and travel to a land God would show him. The first thing therefore that God asked of Abram was an act of trust, a gesture of personal commitment.

If it was true for Abraham, it is equally true for us.

We must leave something to follow God, detach ourselves from someone to respond to our call; we must go; and this runs counter to our idle ways and lazy habits.

It is not easy to go when we do not know where we are going, and it is painful to leave loved ones behind. But go we must if we are to respond fittingly to a God who says: Trust Me and Me only.

After that comes the promise:

'I will make a Covenant between myself and you and increase your numbers greatly.' Abram bowed to the ground and God said this to him: 'Here now is my covenant with you: you shall become the father of a multitude of nations. You shall no longer be called Abram; your name shall be Abraham, for I make you father of a multitude of nations. I will make you most fruitful. I will make you into nations, and your issue shall be kings. I will establish my Covenant between myself and you, and your ancestors after you, generation after generation, a Covenant in perpetuity, to be your God and the God of your descendants after you. I will give to you and to your descendants after you the land you are living in, the whole land of Canaan, to own in perpetuity, and I will be your God.'

(Gn 17:2–8)

A promise like this would have meant little to me. I have never wished to be the father of peoples. But to Abram, who so much wanted a son, the promise meant everything, it was the answer to his deepest longings.

How true it is that God creates in us the desire and the satisfaction, the thirst and the quenching stream!

Yahweh dealt kindly with Sarah as he had said and did what he had promised her. So Sarah conceived and bore a son to Abraham in his old age, at the time God had promised. Abraham named the son born to him Isaac, the son to whom Sarah had given birth.

(Gn 21:1–3)

Isaac, son of the promise, grew up among the tents and flocks of the old patriarch. This father's joy, this fruit of his power for love, was as beautiful as a new-born lamb, as pure as milk, and Abraham was moved when he thought of him, his heart jumped for joy. When the great test came, the terrible trial to Abraham's faith, God had only to choose that flimsy piece of flesh.

There was nothing Abraham held dearer than that. God asked for it as the supreme treasure.

It happened some time later that God put Abraham to the

33

test. 'Abraham, Abraham,' he called. 'Here I am,' he replied. 'Take your son,' God said, 'your only child Isaac, whom you love, and go to the land of Moriah. There you shall offer him as a burnt offering, on a mountain I will point out to you.'

(Gn 22:1–2)

Everything is clear to the believer, everything logical to the man who loves God; a person who is used to listening to 'the voice' has only to obey. Abraham did. We must.

There will be a moment in our vocation when we shall be put to the test, when each of us will undergo, with mortal risk, an extreme trial which engages the whole man to the roots of his being.

Never is a man more of a man than at that moment, never more in God's hands than in that test. To lose that chance of loving is to lose almost all life's value. The very universe is agog to know how man will answer his eternal God.

Rising early next morning Abraham saddled his ass and took with him two of his servants and his son Isaac. He chopped wood for the burnt offering and started on his journey to the place God had pointed out to him. On the third day Abraham looked up and saw the place in the distance. Then Abraham said to his servants, 'Stay here with the donkey. The boy and I will go over there; we will worship and come back to you.'

Abraham took the wood for the burnt offering, loaded it on Isaac, and carried in his own hands the fire and the knife. Then the two of them set out together. Isaac spoke to his father Abraham, 'Father,' he said. 'Yes, my son,' he replied. 'Look,' he said, 'here are the fire and wood, but where is the lamb for the burnt offering?' Abraham answered, 'My son, God himself will provide the lamb for the burnt offering.' Then the two of them went on together.

When they arrived at the place God had pointed out to him, Abraham built an altar there and arranged the wood.

34

Then he bound his son Isaac and put him on the altar on top of the wood. Abraham stretched out his hand and seized the knife to kill his son.

But the angel of Yahweh called to him from heaven. 'Abraham, Abraham,' he said. 'I am here,' he replied. 'Do not raise your hand against the boy,' the angel said. 'Do not harm him, for now I know you fear God. You have not refused me your son, your only son.'

(Gn 22:3–12)

I cannot think of a more beautiful scene than this.

For all time it remains the image and symbol of Calvary, that other hill on which, carrying the wood of His sacrifice, climbed the One whom the Father's love had given for the salvation of men: Jesus.

And it remains the model for all our trials and victories in faith. Sooner or later we too shall have our supreme hour in which God will ask for our reply to His love and will place us naked on the hill of sacrifice.

It will be the most important moment of our existence; it will sum up all the other moments lived in search of our vocation and in the tension of our faith.

Then will come joy, true and lasting peace, the stability of our relationship with God, the fulness of our earthly experiences, the fitting reply to His loving initiative.

Chapter Four

HOPE

If we have found our vocation in faith, we can begin to live it in hope.

Elijah 'walked for forty days and forty nights until he reached Horeb, the mountain of God' (1 K 19:8), just as Israel had wandered for forty years in the desert before gaining access to the Promised Land.

'Forty' in biblical language, does not refer to a specific length of time; it indicates just a long period. We have a long way to go to fulfil our vocation; the end comes only after a period of effort in which we shall need determination, courage and perseverance. As Scripture says: 'Your endurance will win you your lives' (Lk 21:19).

We can, of course, walk without a vocation and therefore without hope, but that is something quite different. If we are walking without hope, our 'sacred history' has not yet begun. Heraclitus said that 'everything is in motion', and the image of history is the river.

However, it is one thing to be swept away by the current, quite another to swim with it. Best of all one can take a boat. Realizing that one is on the river, discovering the purpose of the journey, letting oneself be carried along and rowing against the current are all quite different things.

Birth, life, work, love, death can be regarded as a meaningless fate, or they can become free and joyful acceptance, ecstatic contemplation, a hymn to joy.

The passage from one to the other is brought about by one's

vocation. That is why faith is important. Without faith there are no answers to the questions of life.

Hope continues in time that initial intuition of faith; it is faithfulness to one's vocation, the strength to live it out day by day, the steady gaze on the distant goal right up to the last day of all.

Hope scrutinizes the horizon, fixes in the heart the features and landmarks of the land to be reached. It is faith's memory.

While blind faith contemplates the incomprehensible God and scrutinizes His will in order to fulfil it, hope brings it into time, and to do this it peers as far as the eye can see, way beyond the edge of the desert, beyond the hills of Moab, beyond Mount Nebo from the top of which God showed Moses the Promised Land (Dt 34:1). And if faith is rare and difficult, hope is no less so.

When the people of Israel left Egypt, things were not easy. Moses found himself with the dramatic, frightful and unenviable task of leading through a parched and unknown country a multitude of about 600,000 men, not counting their families (Ex 12:37), who lost heart at each new obstacle, could not understand Moses and his mania for freedom and would have preferred to stay peacefully behind in Egypt where the pots of steaming meat and the rich aroma of roasting onions assailed the nostrils of men who were slaves at heart as well as in fact.

No, it was not easy.

And as it turned out only two men survived the test: Joshua and Caleb. Not even Moses won through: he was buried outside the Promised Land. Two is not many out of 600,000!

The Exodus is the story of a people chosen by God for Himself, and to some extent it serves as the model for all men and therefore for ourselves. Its stages are the stages of our life, its difficulties our difficulties, its hope our hope.

The main obstacle to the hope of the Israelites as they left Egypt was the Sea of Reeds.

It is not easy to trust an invisible and distant God when over one's shoulder, visible and all too near, is the enemy's army and in front an impassable sea.

That the sea would open up was the unlikeliest idea to occur to the people; but that the sea would then close in on the Egyptian army at the exact moment of their crossing – that was something to talk about.

'Then the angel of Yahweh, who marched at the front of the army of Israel, changed station and moved to the rear. The pillar of cloud changed station from the front to the rear of them, and remained there. It came between the camp of the Egyptians and the camp of Israel. The cloud was dark and the night passed without the armies drawing any closer the whole night long. Moses stretched out his hand over the sea. Yahweh drove back the sea with a strong easterly wind all night, and he made dry land of the sea. The waters parted and the sons of Israel went on dry ground right into the sea, walls of water to right and to left of them. The Egyptians gave chase: after them they went, right into the sea, all Pharaoh's horses, his chariots, and his horsemen. In the morning watch Yahweh looked down on the army of the Egyptians from the pillar of fire and of cloud, and threw the army into confusion. He so clogged their chariot wheels that they could scarcely make headway. 'Let us flee from the Israelites,' the Egyptians cried, 'Yahweh is fighting for them against the Egyptians!' 'Stretch out your hand over the sea,' Yahweh said to Moses, 'that the waters may flow back on the Egyptians and their chariots and their horsemen.' Moses stretched out his hand over the sea and, as day broke, the sea returned to its bed. The fleeing Egyptians marched right into it, and Yahweh overthrew the Egyptians in the very middle of the sea. The returning waters overwhelmed the chariots and the horsemen of Pharaoh's whole army, which had followed the Israelites into the sea; not a single one of them was left. But the sons of Israel had marched through the sea on dry ground, walls of water to right and to left of

38

them. That day, Yahweh rescued Israel from the Egyptians, and Israel saw the Egyptians lying dead on the shore. Israel witnessed the great act that Yahweh had performed against the Egyptians, and the people venerated Yahweh; they put their faith in Yahweh and in Moses, his servant.'

(Ex 14:19–31)

It does not need many such episodes to show the believer what God can and does do for His people. One is enough, and the soul can go back to it in meditation any time it needs to.

Our difficulty is not that we find it hard to believe in such a striking and distant fact. Without going so far as to reject it as absurd and impossible – that would take some courage – we can happily consign it to the limbo of religious memories which have nothing to say to our daily life *here and now*.

No, our difficulty is to hope that similar things – on a smaller scale, perhaps! – can still happen in *our* lives, at a moment of particular difficulty.

For example . . .

But then every one of us can furnish examples.

Sooner or later God leads us to our Sea of Reeds. At first He let us play like patriarchal children under the peaceful tents of youth. The spiritual life was easy, we thought we could do anything, we had only to command and our will obeyed.

Then one day . . . like David we saw Bathsheba bathing, like Solomon we were tempted by wealth, like Samson we yielded to Delilah, like Saul we became jealous, like Judas we fell for the purse.

At that moment we discover our true identity; we realize our radical impotence, our infinite illogicality and confusion. We stand on the shores of our Sea of Reeds.

Shattered by temptation, our peace gone, divided in ourselves as if there were two people and two wills instead of one, we suffer all the reverses our arrogance and limitless presumption deserved. And the Sea of Reeds does not open up. Blows fall in quick succession, eating away the very fabric of

39

our humanity; the noble virtues of which we were so proud disintegrate one by one.

> 'I thank you, God, that I am not like the rest of mankind. I fast twice a week; I pay tithes on all I get . . .'
>
> (Lk 18:11–12)

But now we know we *are* like the rest of mankind, all of them.

It is one of the hardest, most humiliating experiences for the person who thinks himself religious to discover how full of wind, how lacking in substance, his religiousness is.

Isaiah, who was not deceived by the religious observances of his people, had some pertinent things to say:

> We were all like men unclean,
> all that integrity of ours like filthy clothing.
> We have all withered like leaves
> and our sins blew us away like the wind.
> You hid your face from us
> and gave us up to the power of our sins.
>
> (64:6–7)

We recognize the truth of these words – in our own lives. And if God did not continually intervene in man's history, the wind of our sinfulness would blow all humanity away like leaves and destroy it in a few generations.

If the Sea of Reeds is a fact and a symbol in the history of our salvation, each of us can find on its banks not just a symbol or a distant fact but a living reality, Jesus Christ, who came to save humanity from its sins.

He is the 'crossing', the 'miracle', the 'strength', the 'sacrament', the 'life', the 'victory', of that Exodus. As man lies gasping on the banks of his own impotence in the chains of his slavery to sin, Christ comes with a cry of hope: 'I have conquered the world' (Jn 16:33).

'I am the Life' (Jn 14:6).

'If any man is thirsty, let him come to me' (Jn 7:38).

'If any one believes in me, even though he dies he will live' (Jn 11:26).

And if man lets the Saviour touch him and has hope, the miracle happens: the sea parts to disclose dry land.

The impossible becomes possible. David sings his Miserere, Samson pays for his sin in tears, Solomon writes his Song of Songs.

Only Judas does nothing; in the mystery of human abjection, he has not allowed the Saviour to heal him.

He hanged himself and died without hope.

Chapter Five

WALKING IN HOPE

Christ is our hope in the fullest sense of that word. When He comes to us in the Sacrament at the fervent wish of our faith, the impossible comes true, impurity vanishes, violence becomes meekness, madness beatitude, death life.

With Jesus charity starts to flow again in the veins of the selfish man trapped in his horrible frozen cave.

From the moment our lives cross His, the thing is done. He is there on all our 'crossings', He Himself becomes our 'crossing', the continuing passover. This is more easily said than done; so much depends on our faith. And without faith . . .

Some people stay on the banks of the Reed Sea all their lives, unable to believe they can ever get across. Enclosed in their own impotence, they cannot believe in God's omnipotence. All they have to do is believe, and they are paralysed by disbelief.

Faith would smash the waters apart, but without it even God's omnipotence is powerless.

How universal this scene is!

No wonder Jesus cried out against men's lack of faith; no wonder He grieved for their obstinacy of heart.

It is difficult to have faith, it is difficult to walk in hope. The Exodus lasted forty years because the people of God found themselves unable to respond to God's love. They preferred to wander in the desert, frightened victims of their own contradictions and fears. God has constantly to ask: 'Is my hand too short to redeem? Have I not strength to save?' (Is 50:2).

He puts this question not only to those who are afraid to take the first step of faith, the crossing from sin to grace, but also to those who have crossed the Reed Sea, who have witnessed the spectacular miracle, who have tasted the joy of liberation, who have looked behind them and seen 'the pick of Pharaoh's horsemen sinking to the bottom of the sea like a stone' (Ex 15:4-5).

In their minds the memory of that crossing has faded. Faced with the need for another act of faith, another act of hope, they are once more in the grip of fear and hope falters.

They are only a few yards from their Lord, but they refuse to feel His healing touch.

If faith does not bubble up, if hope fails, not even Jesus can complete our crossing.

This will go on for forty years, and it is the story of our contradictions.

What a life we make for ourselves!

Why are we so reluctant to believe? Why are we so afraid of trusting in God?

There seem to me to be two main reasons.

1) We have lost our spiritual infancy.

To believe, to be rich in hope, we must be small, as small as infants in their father's arms. Instead we have grown up, become sophisticated, learnt to judge God by the standards of our own essential weakness.

Jesus tells us that unless we change and become like little children we shall never enter the Kingdom of Heaven (Mt 18:3). It is a solemn thought.

This is why spiritual infancy is the secret of making the jump. If we can make ourselves small again we shall be able to believe and hope, and our lives will become simple, unswerving, full.

We must make ourselves small before God, as small as possible, as small as David who believed absolutely that he could not be beaten by Goliath, as small as Joseph who never disputed the angel's orders, as small as Mary who accepted

43

with unswerving simplicity the improbable betrothal of herself and the Spirit of God, the incredible conception within her of Jesus the Christ. 'Blessed is she who believed' (Lk 1:45): therein lies Mary's greatness – and ours too if we learn to believe and hope.

There is no other test of greatness.

Looking at a piece of bread on the altar and saying, 'That is Christ' is pure faith. Noting and listing all the sins of the people of God and its leaders and still letting oneself be guided by the mystery of the Church and its infallibility is a formidable thing; knowing that our bodies rot in the grave and yet believing in the resurrection of the body is a tremendous last test of life.

The successful candidate is the one who has made himself small and does not treat God's mysteries as though they were coins in his pocket.

2) We spend too much time looking backwards; we make no progress on the path of faith because we are too busy looking over our shoulders.

We are thinking of the fleshpots of Egypt, dreaming of the past. Ezechiel reproached the Israelites with hankering after the slavery of Egypt and failing to follow paths laid down by God on Sinai (23:21–31; cf Hos 11:5). We prefer to stay where we are; we are not quite sure God is to be trusted.

His tastes are not to our liking: He gives us manna instead of solid meat, but we do not learn from the experience of the Israelites who were punished for their greed (Nb 11). Our tastes are sensual. We will happily sell our birthright for a plate of soup (Gn 25:29–34); we ask God for wisdom, as Solomon did, but then wallow in lust (1 K 3:8–9; 11:4); we jockey for positions of trust and leadership, but then sell our souls for a vineyard (1 K 21).

It is the same old story. If only we learnt from it that we are no better than others, that we are too happy to drink the water that poisoned our fathers and listen to the Sirens that betrayed our ancestors! God had other things in store for us; He invited us on quite a different adventure:

> 'I will betroth you to myself for ever,
> betroth you with integrity and justice,
> with tenderness and love.'

(Hos 2:21)

It is God who speaks here in words which express the grandeur of His call, the fulness of His love for us.

If only the Virgin of Israel, of whom Jeremiah speaks (18:13) and whom we may take to represent the human soul, would place her hand in God's and, light-footed as a doe and free as a lark, allow God to lead her where He would!

The desert would be crossed in the twinkling of an eye; its solitude would become the ideal place for this infinite love, the bower of a living joy-filled union, the pleasance of the indescribable adventure of love, of our relationship with the eternal, true and infinite God, of our soul's marriage to its gracious Lord!

Instead, what do we find?

Betrayal, adultery, fumbling and hesitation, idolatry, compromises with hell: these lead the soul to the limits of its resistance. Sometimes it looks as if the end has come, and we abandon ourselves to the filthy embrace of Giant Despair.

Hope seems to have been exhausted, only hell is left to listen to our ravings.

Suddenly from the abyss of human misery a force arises which we thought was spent.

It seems to have its origin in the mere instinct for survival, not in a conscious personal act: who can tell where it comes from?

It is a thread of hope!

We start again on the road to the Promised Land.

Chapter Six

LOVE

We are now on the threshold of the great mystery, the source of life, the answer to end all answers: love.

Of what use would faith be on its own? What would be the point of a life lived in hope? What would justify the Exodus, with its discomfort, its long marches, the weariness, thirst and bitter water (Ex 15:22–5), the plague of snakes (Nb 21: 6) and the continual striking camp for new horizons? Love, nothing else.

I set out for love; I am on the move because I am in search of love; I cling to faith and hope because of love.

As St Paul says, 'There are three things that last: faith, hope and love, and the greatest of these is love' (1 Co 13:13).

With light and life love is man's final end and so is identified with God. In John God has defined Himself as Love, and we can therefore confidently assert that our end is love just as we say that our end is God.

And if we look carefully, we shall soon realize that love is a mystery no one can ever define, just like the mystery of God.

We feel love, we experience it, look for it, possess it, but we do not know what it is. Understanding it is beyond us. And yet it 'makes the world go round'! Love is the hinge on which the universe revolves.

Nature comes to life in spring, the flowers burgeon, the animals move, mankind walks – all for love. If it were not for love, the earth would be a lifeless desert, birds would not mate, vegetables would not reproduce, man would remain a lonely being. Without love the universe is unthinkable!

46

We human beings, however, who share in the life of the created world and therefore in all the different kinds of mineral, vegetable and animal love, are also called to share the life of the uncreated world, the divine life.

While here below we live through our earthly spring and smile at the seasons of time, fulfilling ourselves, urged on by the created love which moves us to food or war, to human kindness, to created good, the divine generosity is at work and the movement towards uncreated love – God – begins. In theological language this movement is called 'charity'; it is the supernatural love for God which begins on earth and is completed in total, eternal union with God hereafter. From birth to death man the microcosm experiences all the degrees of created love, but they cannot ever satisfy him. He knows they are not enough. There is an emptiness in him which cannot be filled by earthly love alone. There is a divinely established tension or drive to a love which is not created, which like God is infinite, eternal, transcendent.

Man thus constituted lives on earth but yearns for heaven; he chooses a wife and is still alone, gives life to children and moves through life unaccompanied. There is something in him which remains unsatisfied, which makes him restless, a perpetual seeker.

He is like a pole looking for the other pole, an abyss in search of another abyss.

Augustine said that the heart was restless until it rested in God (*Confessions* 1, 1, 1). This uncreated Love, this Lover distant but near, this reality which is unknown and yet known already is the goal of man's aspirations, searchings and desires. It is God.

Man gropes for God, and God is a love worthy of man. God is repletion, fulness, satiety, peace, joy, happiness – man's last end and total fulfilment.

Whether it is created or uncreated, every kind of love accomplishes a union or marriage and at that moment gives satisfaction, joy, peace, possession – of a kind. The hungry man looks for food, becomes one with the food and his physical life is satisfied; one heart looks for another and friendship results, one body looks for another and gives birth to life, the mind looks for the truth, finds it and experiences joy; man looks for God, unites himself with God and enters eternal life.

The love of a man and his wife is the clearest image of a universal phenomenon, from chemical reactions to the rotation of the stars, from the life of flowers to the nesting of birds, from the mystic's prayer to the uncreated Trinity.

The Bible calls the history of salvation, Israel's journey from slavery in Egypt to freedom in the Promised Land, a sort of betrothal between the Chosen People and the God of Abraham, the mystical marriage of Israel and Yahweh. The prophets are full of it: Isaiah (54:4–8), Jeremiah (2:2), Ezechiel (16:8), Hosea (2:21) all call God Israel's Spouse. The Song of Songs is the wonderful account of the love between God and His people and, ultimately, since the people is an abstract entity, between God and the human soul. God is the soul's Spouse and says to it:

> How beautiful you are, my love,
> how beautiful you are!
> Your eyes, behind your veil,
> are doves;
> your hair is like a flock of goats
> frisking down the slopes of Gilead.

(Sg 4:1)

He adds:

> You ravish my heart,
> my sister, my promised bride,
> you ravish my heart
> with a single one of your glances,
> with one single pearl of your necklace.

(Sg 4:9)

And the soul replies:

48

Let him kiss me with the kisses of his mouth.
Your love is more delightful than wine;
delicate is the fragrance of your perfume,
your name is an oil poured out,
and that is why the maidens love you.
Draw me in your footsteps and let us run.

(Sg 1:2–4a)

If only the world knew these things! If only it knew that the search for God is the greatest adventure of love!

If only it could see that the saint is not an escapist but someone who has realized where true love is and will not rest until he has found it!

Yes, the saint has understood before anyone else. He takes a decision, forges ahead towards his goal, impatient with delay: he wants to anticipate Heaven here on earth!

Then after him comes everybody else, including ourselves – at least I hope so, because there is no other way, there is no other goal.

Most people need a longer apprenticeship. They find difficulty in believing that God is right, they wish to see for themselves and in the process get burnt, dirtied, poisoned and discouraged.

Many begin to see the light at the end of their earthly pilgrimage; many more do not begin to until they are in purgatory, the Kingdom of Silence, meditating on their lives, accepting expiation or purification for their errors and cowardice, undergoing the slow and penetrating fire of charity which rids the soul of all disordered attachments, egoism, pride, falsehood, idols.

There is no other possibility . . . unless . . . no, I cannot bear to think of it, let me contemplate love, let me imagine that all of us will believe in love in the end.

All roads lead to God, to contemplation of the Divine Majesty, to possession of the divine goodness. God is waiting for us; He has been longing for the return of His prodigal son.

Chapter Seven

THE PATH OF LOVE

If there had been no sin, things would have been simple, or so at least we limited mortals, victims of sin, like to think.

Man would have steered the course of his life, from the dawn to the twilight of his earthly existence, straight towards God, confidently, without being led astray by will-o'-the-wisps.

The seasons of life, the possession of creatures, the partial vision of things in time would not have obstructed the eternal season of God, the possession of the Absolute and the contemplation of the Transcendent.

Facts are facts, however. There was a break, and nothing has turned out as it might have done.

Here is not the place to embark on the how and why of sin. I am not a theologian, and the theologians have not fully convinced me: there is always something which exceeds our ability to understand . . .

I simply accept the matter. There has been a break, and none of us can doubt it; no one can fail to taste its bitter reality.

Is there anyone who does not feel that *within himself* all is not well?

That there is something wrong, unmanageable, disordered, evil, sick? Who among us does not feel that from the chasm of our being a pestilential miasma rises up, that – to change the image – a twisted, barren root, which withstands the axe of our will and proliferates in our stony field after a single night of inactivity or an hour of inattentiveness on our part, emerges triumphantly from the impoverished soil?

Evil is real, fearfully real, and our existential experience of life is more than enough to convince us of this, certainly more than theological considerations, even though these are accurate (if partial because of our limitations). It is in living and growing old that we perceive the truth about sin, that first calamitous break with God, and feel its seriousness and constant presence.

There is no cancer, however malignant, no septicaemia, no leprosy however frightful which can compare with the gravity and horror of evil.

The people who have had the clearest insight into it are not the hardened sinners filthy with sin but the saints, after years of struggle with it. They blanched merely to think of the obscenities, revolts, blasphemies, violence, evil and perversion it could cover. But even their view was limited.

The face of Jesus – the authentic, unique Saint – went as white as a corpse in the Garden of Olives and then 'his sweat fell to the ground like great drops of blood' (Lk 22:44).

Jesus suffered an agony of soul to see evil – sin, a thick and horrifying crust covering Him – as the Just Judge, the Father of eternal love, saw it at the divine Tribunal.

What a terrible thing sin is, man's rebellion against God, saying no to Love! We cannot really understand it; and therefore we cannot properly understand hell. Hell baffles us: we cannot conceive or express it, our minds are not big enough.

Jesus, however, *could* understand it, and that is why He suffered all a man can suffer and did not flinch from flinging into the scales the whole weight and value of His sacrifice. Our bitter experience of sin's consequences in our life, our many betrayals will perhaps have helped to give us some understanding.

What a tragic vision we should then have of human reality in history: from the Hiroshima bomb to the hunger of the Third World, from populations uprooted by hate and immured in concentration camps to the racial and social turpitude of all centuries, from the Pharisaism of the rich to the

51

debasement of the poor, from the disintegration of the family to the boredom of wealth, from the fading smiles of children to the desperation of the old!

Do not tell me that war is inevitable, or that the world cannot produce enough food for everybody, or that certain races are destined to dominate and others to serve, or that life is life and man cannot escape the law of the jungle.

No, evil is evil, sin is sin, and the biblical image of a forbidden fruit wrenched from the grasp of a loving God in disobedience to His will is the prototype of a reality none of us can dispute because we experience it for ourselves in the depths of our own being.

Yes, I am capable of treating my brothers as Hitler treated the Jews, of dropping not one but a thousand atomic bombs, of committing any sin. I know, because experience has told me.

There is no sin in the world that I have not committed or am incapable of committing, and so we are all one in Adam, and the tragic tree of Eden is the tree of reality under which we rest from the noonday sun while the devil prowls around like a roaring lion looking for someone to eat (1 P 5:8). How true the Bible is!

Our only course is to accept things as they are and start again at the foot of the slope.

Step by step we must retrace the path. Expelled from Paradise for disobeying love, we must return by loving.

Love is the surest guide. This time, you see, Jesus is our leader.

Just as human nature fell in an act of disobedience, so salvation came in Christ's act of obedience. It was not Jesus's sufferings which redeemed humanity so much as His inner attitude of love and obedience to the Father, which was obedience to Light, Love and Being.

We must climb the slope again even though it will not be easy and even though at every corner there is a wild beast to chase us back.

With our hand in Jesus's hand and our eyes on His, we must walk towards the Promised Land as members of God's people.

When I say that it is love that must guide us, I mean all of love.

We must not make the mistake of separating love into human and divine and then concentrating on the latter to the neglect of the former. That would be mistaken zeal.

Jesus Himself told us that the second commandment, which is like the first, enjoins us to love our neighbour as ourself and that the whole Law hangs on these two commandments (Mt 22:39-40). Too often people deceive themselves that they can separate love of God from love of one's neighbour. We are all familiar with the 'disembodied' religious zealot who looks for God and is harsh with his fellows, who takes refuge in prayer and lets his neighbour die of starvation.

He is deluding himself!

Love cannot be divided. If it is genuine it serves God *and* the neighbour in the same act. Or better, it sees God in the neighbour and the neighbour in the heart of God.

This proper balance or identity is not easy to achieve; it is extremely uncomfortable for one thing. But today perhaps more than ever before, when we are more aware of the world's unity and reject with vigour and disgust a Christianity which separates adoration of God from His presence in suffering humanity, the effort must be made.

God is in the man to be saved, and the man to be saved is in God's thoughts. The commandment of love embraces both poles of this relationship.

> Anyone who says, 'I love God',
> and hates his brother,
> is a liar.

> (1 Jn 4:20)

If a man who was rich enough in this world's goods
saw that one of his brothers was in need,

53

but closed his heart to him,
how could the love of God be living in him?

(1 Jn 3:17)

Love of God goes hand in hand with love of one's fellow men. We love God in our neighbour and our neighbour in God. And if we do, we are moving towards our full realization as persons in Jesus Christ.

There is a story which I particularly like because it expresses all this so wonderfully. It is the story of St Christopher.

St Christopher – so this story goes – was a giant of a man, a pagan, converted by a hermit. He had great difficulties in prayer: he could not convince himself that God was really there. He became discouraged with the hours of fasting and psalms and kept on asking his mentor when he would see the face of God. The hermit realized that it was premature to force his new pupil to undergo the dryness of prayer and so suggested an easier, more 'human', programme. He asked him whether he knew of a river not far away which travellers found very difficult to cross.

> 'Because thou art noble and high of stature and strong in thy members thou shalt be resident by that river, and thou shalt bear over all them that shall pass there.'

This was equivalent to saying that the face of God was still not clear to Christopher in naked faith and that he would therefore find it in the people he served.

So, equipped with a massive staff, Christopher set to work, day after day, bearing pilgrims across the river . . . until one day he carried over Jesus in the form of a small child. At that moment the pagan giant became Christ-Bearer and discovered the face of God.

Our situation is like that of Christopher. Working and loving our work, building up our family, being part of society

54

and trying to make it happier and juster, loving things, all things, as messages of God, we gradually climb the steps of love to reach up to God.

And when we manage to break through the human, earthly wrapping of life, when we finally succeed in puncturing the appearances that surround us, we shall understand that our efforts to be faithful to love, our patience in bearing ourselves and others have been instrumental in drawing us up to the pure and eternal love of God.

PART II

As we said in the first part, we should not draw any distinction between love for God and love for our neighbour. Both these loves must be lived out together and welded into a single whole.

There are two schools, both created by God for our benefit, which, with steady training, can help us to do this: the family and work.

In the following seven meditations we shall be thinking about these two things.

Chapter Eight

IT IS NOT GOOD THAT THE MAN
SHOULD BE ALONE

God is not 'alone', because He is a Trinity. If there were only one Person in God, He would be a solitary figure. God is not solitary: He is Love, and Love is the opposite of solitude.

God is Three in One, and this is a beautiful thing to be able to say; if it were not so, we should understand nothing of God. Perfection does not consist in being one Person in one nature; perfection consists in being three Persons in the unity of a single nature, and God is this perfection.

The mystery of the Trinity is the most beautiful thing we can contemplate and with the mystery of the Incarnation of the Word gives us more than enough to sustain us on our long journey towards Love.

I spend hours on end contemplating these two mysteries, and I never tire of it. I often weep with love and experience an inexpressible longing.

I think of the Father's face, I am enraptured by Jesus's face, I contemplate the face of the Holy Spirit: I believe they are the same thing, but that is a revelation only He can give and He gives it to the creature who asks in love: 'O Lord, reveal Yourself to me.'

The three divine Persons wrapped in the mystery of Their incomprehensibility reveal themselves to me in prayer, and I have no more passionate wish than to deepen my knowledge of Them.

This is eternal life, which we already possess here on earth if we do the Father's will. 'Eternal life is this', said Jesus, 'to know you, the only true God, and Jesus Christ whom you have sent' (Jn 17:3).

A single Person in God would be inconceivable. He would not be God because He would be sad, and God is joy, supreme joy.

God explodes from within the explosive heart of love: He cannot be contained. The person who loves knows what I mean by this and will bear me out. The created universe is under the sign of this explosiveness, this growth, this expansion. They say that it is growing and that new stars are continually being born.

I do not know what God could add which would explain His explosive, loving, creative nature better to us.

Everything speaks to me of this love, this gift, this diffusion of Himself.

From the stars to the flowers, from chemical reactions to the beasts of the field, from the cosmos to man, the command to 'be fruitful and multiply' is stamped into the nature of things, it is the rhythm of the universe, it is the hymn of the galaxies and of young couples going to the altar.

When God looked at the man He had just created, He said: 'It is not good for the man to be alone', and He provided a companion: woman. The creation of woman is beautifully told in Genesis:

> Yahweh God made the man fall into a deep sleep. And while he slept, he took one of his ribs and enclosed it in flesh. Yahweh God built the rib he had taken from the man into a woman, and brought her to the man.
>
> (Gn 2:21–2)

As always in the Bible, the truth is concealed beneath symbols and the signs of words. Adam's sleep is like an ecstasy in which the man sees and loves and desires the creature for whom he searches and whom God Himself offers, the creature who suits him, who will complete him, who will gladden him, who will help him to make the most of himself.

And waking up he sees this creature and exclaims: 'This at last is bone from my bones, and flesh from my flesh' (Gn 2:23).

The biblical account of the creation of woman reads almost like a children's story. It is one, in fact, because basically man will always be 'God's child', and here it is God talking. But it has such a ring of truth about it that beyond the signs of the words there lies the mystery of the deep, unbreakable union of man and woman.

It is God's intention that they should be 'chips off the same block', so that metaphysically a man will not be able to say to a woman: 'Go away, I don't know you, you and I don't belong together.'

No, he will always have to say: 'Bone from my bones, flesh from my flesh' and remain with her; as long as life lasts, he cannot separate himself from his own flesh.

Man therefore must be united with his wife: God wanted it to be like this, and so should we.

'It is not good for the man to be alone': these are strong words. If God says so, there can be no doubt: 'It is not good.'

To live his life properly man must marry. He cannot say too lightly, 'No, I shan't get married, I'll stay on my own.' He would commit a sin if he did, because sin is disobedience to God, to God's will.

Except for higher motives (to which we shall return shortly) or because of some evident impediment (incapacity, illness, destitution), man on earth must obey God's invitation and bear those clear words constantly in mind: 'It is not good . . . it is not good . . . it is not good.'

Why do I put so much emphasis on this?

Because it is necessary to do so. Some men believe they can renounce marriage for no good reason; some suffer from the erroneous conviction that marriage is not one of the most important things in life.

Some even exclude marriage simply because it is not convenient, others for trivial reasons such as not wishing to share their property.

61

No, to live his life properly a man must marry.

Woman completes man, and man woman. Love fulfils them, makes them better, introduces them more easily into the divine stream of charity, forces them to become open, transforms them.

And it also makes them fruitful. We have said that fecundity is stamped into the nature of things as a sign of God's creativeness, and man is no exception.

Marriage makes man a father and woman a mother, and so sublime is this miracle that we should kneel when we speak of it.

When a father gazes into the innocent eyes of his son, he will, if he looks carefully, see the mystery of the infinite, of the unfathomable, of the ungraspable. He will feel that even though this little body belongs to him, because it was born from his blood, it comes from a distant world, from infinity, from God. God created him at the very moment when man desired a son and in the unity of love saw him as it were issuing forth from the chaos of non-being.

For an instant man has shared in God's creative joy and has touched the infinite. Whenever love is lived to the full, man feels he is touching God, and this is the sole moment in which man on earth can say exultantly, 'For ever'.

People often talk of children as if they were encumbrances, matrimonial 'accidents', undesirable.

Of course, if we are wrapped up in ourselves we shall understand nothing of the fulness of love. We shall look only for the pleasure, and the marriage is organized and calculated with a view to excluding children.

Birth control can be a virtue, a noble sacrifice, a real necessity, but when it is motivated by the egoism of the rich and healthy – who are its main practitioners – it becomes a perversion.

The person who decides to have no more children has left the trajectory of God's explosiveness and is like a rotten branch waiting to consummate its uselessness on the bonfire.

I can understand that a young couple may be obliged to limit the size of their family because of the wife's health, for example, or because they are destitute, or for some other perfectly valid reason arising out of the difficulties of life today, but I cannot see how they could possibly do so with a smile, happy in the knowledge that they have found a means of deceiving life.

No, it is a great sorrow, a sadness, not to see the face of a child that should have been born but now will never be.

A normal, healthy, decent man who still retains some feeling for God should want children, a lot of children. A woman even more so.

Pharisaism, which has been with us in every age, urges us, almost unconsciously, to put a higher value on the sexual act than on the intention, and in some people's morality the only worry is to avoid contravening the law.

Because everything has been done according to the letter of the law, with a calendar in hand, some couples manage to have no children without offending morality; but the result is an unfruitful life.

And if their lives are unfruitful, who will save them from judgement?

Will God analyse their acts and overlook their lives?

Will he not rather call them 'hypocrites', as Jesus called the Pharisees, or better still, 'whitened sepulchres'?

Chapter Nine

LIFE TOGETHER

The purpose of marriage, however, is not only to give birth to children – although that on its own is a thing of divine beauty. It is also designed to fulfil the marriage partners. The matrimonial union does not concern only the generation to come: it should also be seen as a divinely willed means to fulfil, reconcile, cheer, sustain, improve the man and the woman.

This fulfilment is brought by love, it is realized in love.

Here we could apply Augustine's famous 'love and do what you like', in the certainty that if the partners really love each other they will find in their mutual relationship the path, the pointer, the ladder to another love which should develop in every creature on earth and take it later to perfect union with God. I should say that matrimonial love – for those whose vocation is marriage, that is, for most of mankind – is the beginning, the pattern, the blueprint, of love for the Absolute in which, beyond time, we shall all be absorbed.

Marriage partners who love each other find that love synthesizes their relationship. Life together becomes easy in love; it becomes easy to understand, bear with and excuse each other. It even becomes easy to sacrifice oneself for the other.

Love in marriage ultimately helps a man to leave the dark cave of his egoism and the constant danger of returning to himself and to become open to creation and so to God. I have seen impossible youths – timid, introvert, unmanageable – suddenly become gentle, open, altruist in the warmth of a girlfriend's love. It is like seeing a dead branch fill with sap and bud at the approach of spring.

Love is an all-the-year-round spring!

We can never sufficiently express the benefits of love, especially on the sick, the timid, pessimists, egoists, difficult cases.

No medicine is so powerful as genuine love.

Everything mends and comes to life; and instead of lapsing into an empty, sterile melancholy, we set off with enthusiasm as if life had started to flow through our veins again.

Saved by love, we find in it the joy of life, application to our work, dedication to an ideal, and under its inspiration we can at last devote our lives to something worthwhile!

Love, truth, is God's finger laid on man's heart.

Furthermore, such an intimate and radical life for two as marriage imposes sets man on the path to self-discovery. In his partner's eyes he sees himself as in a mirror, with all his mystery and unfathomable depth.

It is fatal if love does not survive this discovery. We have to realize that in ourselves we find not only positive aspects but negative aspects too. We uncover weakness, limitation, mediocrity and even, unfortunately, evil. At this moment a new love, more mature, more realistic, more subtle, must come to the fore: we mean *mercy*, *compassion*, a degree of love which should fill the waning years of our life on earth.

It is all too easy to love one's partner when she is young and wrapped in mystery; much more difficult when one discovers her ugliness, limitations, slovenliness, egoism. If a man cannot survive the crisis precipitated by this discovery with the love of mercy, he is sowing the seeds of future difficulties; he is entering a tragic stage in his marriage.

If, on the other hand, he remains true to his love and sees his own sin and weakness in his partner's, he becomes accustomed to facing the truth, and his life enters a new phase animated no longer by feeling or emotion but by true and genuine love.

Then, when the family has grown to three or more, the school of love takes on an unsuspected, almost total plenitude. There are times – unfortunately rare because original sin is an ever-present reality – when we begin to wonder whether Heaven has not come down to earth.

The father-mother-child relationship approaches the summit of love.

It is a competition to feel others' lives more precious than one's own, and, to be faithful to this stimulus, we can – albeit still on a natural plane – approach the degree of love Jesus showed and which He called in the Gospel 'His commandment'.

'Just as I have loved you, you also must love one another' (Jn 13:34), that is, to the point of sacrificing one's life, which is the highest degree of love. And here I must make my confession: I was unprepared under the great rock when I dreamt I was dead and was being judged by God. As I told the reader earlier, I had abandoned the world and my affairs to look for God alone. I had gone into the desert to strip myself and to learn to love those poorer than myself. And yet on the night it was cold, I denied a poor old man a blanket. I was afraid of shivering in the night.

Would you believe it? To show me my own insignificance and to coax me into the ways of that truth which we call humility, God lay in wait for me.

Some months after the episode of the blanket which I had refused to give to Kadà – the poor man in the desert – a medical lieutenant of the Foreign Legion said to me: 'Brother Carlo, if you are going to Tazrouk, visit the camps at Uksem: there you will see some really poor people.' Without thinking that God was trying to teach me something new, I set out to visit the camps as soon as an opportunity presented itself.

I arrived at dawn one morning and it was still cold. I was taken near a tent apart from the others in which a woman was dying.

She was a black slave, unmarried but with a tiny little boy.

I went into the tent and stood aghast at the indescribable squalor.

66

The poor woman was lying on a mat of dried grass, shivering. Her only bedclothing was a piece of blue cotton cloth (blue being the typical colour of the Tuareg tribe who 'employed' her). It was in tatters and could have afforded her no warmth. At her side lay the child in half a woollen blanket.

Even in the face of death, this poor woman had preferred to go cold while her child had all the warmth she could offer.

She was not a Christian, her 'employers' forced her into prostitution, she counted as absolutely nothing, she was dying as the real poor of the Third World die. But she had expressed perfect love for her son: she had loved him to the point of sacrifice and with such simplicity as if it had been a matter of course, a thing of no importance.

I felt as dry as the sand in the desert, humiliated by a divine sublimity which this woman had lived in unadorned nature but which I had not learnt in the superiority of grace.

God was there in that infinitely poor tent. He had managed to persuade that person, loved and respected by no one, to accept an act worthy of Jesus's love on Calvary: the simple, unprotesting gift of self.

Chapter Ten

THIS IS WEAKNESS, NOT LOVE!

It is evening, any one of countless typical evenings.

Dad has come home from work and is now happily reading his newspaper comfortably ensconced in an armchair. Mum is in the kitchen preparing the evening meal, and every so often, taking care not to interrupt unnecessarily, she asks how the day went or gives her own small items of daily news from the neighbourhood.

The atmosphere is peaceful and relaxed.

Until . . .

An intruder enters the camp.

Two feet high and still uncertain whether to be a biped or a quadruped, he leaves his corner where he has been engrossed in smashing the last of the toys showered on him by doting parents, crawls over to his father's chair and with a wild snatch rips the paper from his father's grasp.

The room is charged with tension. Mum interrupts her work to remove the little nuisance and take him back to his toy (thrown to the wild beast, dedicated to the sacrifice, for love of peace). 'Come on, you naughty little thing,' says Mum in a vague tone, 'leave Daddy's paper alone.'

Dad patiently gathers up the bits, looks at his wife as if to say that it is all her fault for not training the child properly and then resumes his reading.

Not many minutes go by – just enough for the toddler to summon up strength again – and here he is crawling towards the evening's prey: Daddy's paper.

There comes another tug, more eyes raised in exasperation, another quick lift back to the corner.

It is evident that the peace is ended and war declared, no holds barred. On one side there is a combatant who wants to win and knows he can, on the other two combatants who are at their wits' end and wish just to establish a truce.

This time the attack recommences immediately, without even a pause for breath. It being such fun to pull, the little horror tugs on the end of the tablecloth.

The result: three broken glasses, a lot of noise and, much more serious, the shattering of that fragile peace.

'Can't you control that child . . . I come home after a hard day's work and all you can do . . .'

'Now look here, I have him all day long, you don't help, and instead of taking an interest in the child you simply go out in the evening.'

'Right, I'm going.'

And he has a snack in a café.

My only wish is for that young couple, victims of an age like our own in which the institution of authority has crumbled, in which parents bring their children up like savages for fear of creating complexes, in which, out of a mistaken concept of love, they no longer have the courage to administer punishment, to read quietly to themselves this passage from the Bible:

A man who loves his son will beat him frequently
    so that in after years the son may be his comfort.
A man who is strict with his son will reap the benefit,
    and be able to boast of him to his acquaintances.
A man who educates his son will be the envy of his enemy,
    and will be proud of him among his friends.
A horse badly broken-in turns out stubborn,
    an uncontrolled son turns out headstrong.
Pamper your child, and he will give you a fright,
    play with him, and he will bring you sorrow.

Allow him no independence in childhood,
   and do not wink at his mistakes.
Bend his neck in youth,
   bruise his ribs while he is a child,
or else he will grow stubborn and disobedient,
   and hurt you very deeply.
Be strict with your son, and persevere with him,
   or you will rue his insolence.

(Si 30:1–3, 8–9, 11–13)

These are the words of Eternal Wisdom, because the Bible is the word of God, and even if we have to interpret them, bring them down to our level, which is not high, and apply them to our situation, which is always unstable and mutable, we cannot fail to find in this passage a clear, precise exposition of the educational relationship that should exist between parents and their children.

The mentality that has grown up in the last decades, which have been an age of transition from a past that is still not dead to a future that is not yet mature, is decidedly incorrect, or better, unbalanced.

Just as democracy has replaced absolute rule 'from above', an education of 'love' has replaced the authoritarianism of the past.

But since man is by nature unbalanced, he has simply substituted one exaggeration for another. Excessive intransigence has given way to licence; instead of commands there are invitations, instead of punishments caresses.

It was once said that democracy is an appropriate gift to mature peoples, just as freedom is a proper bequest to responsible people.

The mistake, however, is to think that I can offer democracy to the immature, freedom to irresponsible children. The parent has a *duty* to educate, lead by the hand, guide and punish because the child is not mature, he cannot yet do things for himself. His mother and father supply the strength he lacks, the judgement he lacks, the light he has yet to acquire.

The child has a *right* to be educated, supported, corrected, punished. Otherwise there is chaos – for the parents and, worse still, for the child himself.

In the episode with which we began this meditation, what went wrong? In my opinion the mistake lay in the fact that the parents were afraid to make the child suffer; they could not bring themselves to punish him; they were terrified of seeing him cry. It is not that they did not know what to do. Nothing is simpler, especially when the child is three or four. Stay where you are without being a nuisance – play properly as you should do – don't touch this or that – get up, sit down, like this – don't interrupt when others are speaking – and so on.

The trouble starts when parents fail to apply their educational programme: they yield in the face of disobedience, they give in to tantrums, they accept the child's point of view. In short, they adopt the child's programme, which is irrational and arbitrary.

In particular they have no idea how to punish. From a mistaken idea of love, they cannot bear to hear the child cry, they are afraid that punishment is harmful, they think the child should be always smiling and satisfied.

Their mistake here is colossal. The child needs to cry; he longs to be punished, to be bent, to be put right.

Punishment is a solid and nourishing food which he cannot do without: the sense of justice deep in his nature demands it.

Punishment liberates him. It releases the pus from the boils. It makes the child laugh when all is over and the operation is successful.

Listen to the Bible again:

> Do not be chary of correcting a child,
>   a stroke of the cane is not likely to kill him.
> A stroke of the cane
>   and you save him from hell.

(Pr 23:13)

Parents should have the strength to bend their child's sick will because of the love they have for him. It is for love that they must be the masters, he the subject.

Out of love for him they will make him cry.

If they accept the child's will, what are they doing in fact? They are accepting a fatuous, senseless thing, something Scripture calls 'folly':

> Innate in the heart of a child is folly,
> judicious beating will rid him of it.
>
> (Pr 22:15)

How angry I get when I see parents laughing at the stupidities of their children! How can they go along with such senselessness? How can they tolerate such obstinacy and capriciousness? I have witnessed evenings poisoned by the presence of one or two horrible children who, appreciating their parents' weakness, rampage like unchained beasts with the sole purpose of asserting their nascent personalities, vain and empty even at this early stage.

I have seen families in a state of war simply because the children have not been fortunate enough to have a mother or father with an iron fist – or at least a determination and ability to make for a goal which must be reached at all costs.

Let us be quite clear that it is not just a question of punishing, of hitting out, as if education were like rearing cows or mules.

The parents have to achieve what must be achieved, whatever the price.

Some children need only one good hiding all their lives; others might need only a stern look.

The important thing is that the child knows that he and not his parents must give in. This is especially true in infancy, which should be the most favourable age for laying the foundations of a proper education. The French call it the years of *dressage*.

Later, as the child grows, he will be given more responsibility and invited to cooperate instead of just undergoing education – this is particularly true of the crisis of adolescence – but the duties of those who have received from God and nature the mission of leading him to the threshold of maturity are indispensable to the end.

These observations affect not only the education of the children but also the unity and affection of the parents.

Too often the marriage begins to crack, harsh words to be bandied about, simply because of the partners' inability to bring up their children properly or because of their disagreement over how to do so.

'It's up to you.'

'You're just weak.'

'What are you doing while I shout myself hoarse?'

'It's too easy to give orders to us women while you men go off without ever lending a hand.'

And because we are basically sinful, we always end up by blaming the other person.

And in blaming the other person we do not realize that we are digging the first spadefuls of that bottomless pit of evil: lack of love.

Chapter Eleven

MAN AND WORK

As the bird is made to fly and the fish to swim, man is made to work.

Work is man's natural element, and his life on earth would be inconceivable without it. In work he fulfils, completes and expresses himself as well as expressing, fulfilling and completing creation.

We could say that God created a world that was unfinished. He intended to invite man to cooperate with Him in His work of completing creation: man would become God's associate in realizing the divine plan, in making the divine will effective.

By his work man puts the finishing touch to creation, he improves and adorns it.

Take an uncultivated hillside: nothing but brambles, thorn-bushes, twisted trees. There is a wild olive-grove: the leaves are small, dry, the fruit desiccated.

Along comes man.

He seems to caress the trees with his work. He cuts them back, tidies them up, grafts on new stock, manures the ground. After a time the olive leaves have softened, the berries have become succulent, the very branches seem to stretch out at peace, more harmoniously, more truly themselves.

The wild hillside is transformed into a rich olive-yard: the 'after' is better than the 'before'.

We could say that man is not 'alone' in his work, that God Himself works through him: and that is true.

God, immanent in creation, works with creation to effect His plan and makes use of everything, including man.

How mysterious God's work in the world is!

Too often we have an anthropomorphic concept of God; we think of Him in crude physical terms. We imagine Him to be detached from creation, whereas the catechism's phrase to the effect that 'God is immense' should draw our attention to the reality of the situation. God is here, He is there, He is everywhere; He is in me, in the olive-tree, in everything. He is the root of Being, He is the Being in which everything shares.

What a stupendous mystery!

However, returning to our main theme, we can say that God thought and willed man like this and in calling him to life called him to work.

Seen in this 'theological' light, work is indispensable to man because God's plan incorporates it.

God's hand calls to beauty in the hand of the artist; desires the unity of the human family in the hand of the technologue; desires bread for His children in the hand of the workman.

God is in all men's work and in all people of goodwill. No discovery of man's is absent from God's mind, no technological achievement is possible without His divine will for good.

Yes, work is indispensable for man.

It could be objected that prayer, not work, is 'indispensable'. We are made to pray, not to work, it is urged. The objector would like to be thought pious, but in fact he does not realize what he is saying.

His idea of prayer is too abstract, too angelic. The Benedictines, who were great contemplatives, and the Trappists, who are familiar with the strenuous efforts required by prayer, divide the day into three sections: seven hours of work, seven of prayer, seven of sleep.

The rest is devoted to cementing these three sections together.

If a person says that 'we are made for prayer', he is obviously unaware, perhaps because he has never tried it, that one cannot pray for twenty-four hours on end – not, that is, without going mad.

The person who prays, particularly if he prays a lot, needs

75

work to give balance to his day and rest to restore energy to his hours of prayer.

No one can spend all day in church – unless, of course, we wish to produce sick and unbalanced minds.

In the first chapters of Genesis we read: 'The Lord God took the man and settled him in the garden of Eden to cultivate and take care of it' (Gn 2:15).

This brief biblical text is extraordinarily instructive and should be engraved in everyone's thoughts.

A question springs spontaneously to mind: is man obliged to work? The answer is clear and applies universally. Except for very special reasons, man is obliged to work. God gave man work before sin, when the earth was still a 'garden of Eden' and Adam was still at peace with himself and with God.

God's original plan was for man 'to cultivate and take care of' the land. In His Wisdom He decreed at the very beginning: 'Let us make man in our own image . . . let them be masters of the fish of the sea, the birds of heaven, the cattle, all the wild beasts and all the reptiles that crawl upon the earth' (Gn 1:26).

The command is unmistakable, and ignorance of the texts is no excuse for excluding it from our lives.

If someone says, 'My father has left me a considerable fortune; I've enough to live on for the rest of my life and so I needn't work; in fact I shan't work, I shall live a life of total ease', is he justified? No, he is not. He is in a state of sin, continual sin. Work is not merely a means of earning bread and butter with which one may dispense if there are alternative sources of income, it is much more: it is a divine commandment, a service to humanity, a duty of man on earth and finally, as we shall see, a redemption from sin.

Our puritan and bourgeois education is a funny thing: we're terrified of seeing our daughter come home pregnant.

But we rarely ask her: are you working? have you made yourself useful today? are you an idle little teenager spending God's hours listening to records on the bed, just killing time?

In this we have to admit that we are the heirs of an age in which Christianity itself was infected by pagan culture and a pagan mentality.

The nobles, even Christian nobles, considered work unworthy of their lineage, and the rich bourgeoisie regarded it as no more than an instrument for accumulating wealth.

Of course they never wondered whether they were free not to work because they had no need of money; whether they could live on private income and be obligated to no one!

I have to say that I have never heard a sermon in church against those who live on private means even though they are young and fit!

But I was saying that even the Christians' way of life has been infected by the pagan attitudes of previous eras.

Let me give you an example which caused me much grief during the critical period of the worker-priest experiment. With my own ears I heard from informed Christians phrases such as 'The priest should not be working. It will damage his dignity.' Sentiments like this reveal the extent to which the mentality of the pagan world has infiltrated the Christian ranks and the extent to which we have departed from the evangelical spirit.

How could someone with the effrontery to speak like this never have paused to consider that Jesus, the Eternal Priest, spent thirty years doing manual work? Was that beneath His dignity?

What does dignity depend on anyway? Expensive clothes? A fat bank balance?

My Jesus, how far have Your followers wandered from Your example!

They forget that You, Son of the Most High, bridge between heaven and earth, the most extraordinary Man who has ever lived on earth, eternal judge, Incarnate Word, did work with Your hands which they would consider beneath Your priestly dignity!

What a terrible thought!

77

Chapter Twelve

WITH SWEAT ON YOUR BROW
SHALL YOU EAT YOUR BREAD

An aspect of work we have yet to consider is that it is *redemptive*.

If it is true that work is the means by which man participates in God's creative work, an instrument of harmony and beauty, the fulfilment of wonderful plans all contributing to the unity and happiness of the human family, it is also, and will remain so until the end of time, 'redemptive'.

Not for nothing did God tell Adam after his sin: 'With sweat on your brow shall you eat your bread' (Gn 3:19).

Before the disorder introduced by sin, work was a joy; sin brought effort, suffering, toil. From then on work has been redemptive, helping man to free himself from evil, to pay his debts with justice, to be responsible and useful, to collaborate day after day in his own salvation. And here I am not talking to those whose work is governed by the harsh necessity of procuring 'daily bread', especially when it is scarce and uncertain.

I feel unworthy to do so, especially now that I witness the daily drama of poverty as a Little Brother among the poorest of the poor. I have seen people who have had no choice (and that is perhaps the most painful part of it) but are forced by penury to take any work left on the market: heavy, dirty, badly paid, brutalizing. I have seen men at the bottom of mines crucified by the dust that corrodes the lungs and the continual damp which swells the joints and leads to old age at forty! men bent under the African and Asian sun, on the roads or in shipyards, with picks and shovels which hour by hour become instruments of torture, under-nourished, dirty, joyless, living in lonely huts at night far from their wives and children. How you redeem the world, you poor workers! How you bear the heavy privilege of the cross!

No, I shall not speak to you. I am lost in admiration, and I kneel before such suffering! I shall speak instead, in your name, to those who are not forced to work for their daily bread, either because they have enough money in the bank or because they receive enough charity, and I should like to remind them, in the name of the others, that the Lord's command to work applies to everyone, including them.

You cannot exempt yourselves merely because you have no need of food. Blood corroded and poisoned by sin flows in *your* veins too, and nothing is more harmful to virtue and Christian asceticism than idleness and ease, nothing more hurtful to holiness than sloth. If you do not make an effort, if your brow does not sweat, you cannot live the Gospel: do not delude yourselves! Do not try to escape the cross: you cannot!

In many Catholic circles today, there is a sort of panic in the face of the difficulties of the young to fulfil their vocation or resist temptation or live in charity. The young sit for hours on end with their bottoms glued to a chair in front of the television, they get up as late as possible in the morning, they live lives which lack nothing and from which sacrifice is totally absent, and they expect the problems of the evangelical life to be solved! How can they be? Is Jesus's teaching no longer applicable today? 'Anyone who does not carry his cross and come after me cannot be my disciple' (Lk 14:27) – does this not apply to the Christians of wealthy countries? of the well-off continents? I have no hesitation in asserting that consumer society is a far greater danger to the Christianity of our time than communism, which is much deprecated and combated. Even though communism might impose its hard cross on men and deprive them of their freedom, it might do less harm to a way of life which, because it is based on hedonism and opulence and banishes the cross completely from people's homes and from the streets, threatens to deaden Christians' wills and turn Christians into baptized pagans.

We must keep watch and be vigilant. This means respecting God's word.

Only God's word does not pass!

And if God tells us that we must eat with 'sweat on our brow', well, we have to make sure we do.

Can an athlete hope to breast the tape without effort? Can a champion hope to win if he is not prepared to sweat for it? And is virtue easier than a race? charity more easily attainable than an athletic prize?

Modern civilization has taken away the sweat of previous centuries with its scientific advances. The car enables us to avoid tiring journeys on foot, the washing-machine the drudgery of scrubbing clothes, the aeroplane tedious journeys by train or boat: we no longer raise a sweat.

The Christian, however, who knows he must sweat, looks for new ways of doing so, so as not to escape the Lord's warning.

Why should cleaners and domestics be employed in colleges and seminaries and religious houses to sweep, wash and serve?

Even in novitiates I have seen the novices waited on by poor people who are often very badly paid. It is anti-Christian and a scandal.

Would it not be much better to share the work out among the young men themselves, accustom them to tidying their own rooms, keeping the house clean, organizing their meals, peeling potatoes?

Of course they would lose out on aesthetics, but they would gain in humility and charity.

A religious community has to find work for its members to keep the spirit in training and preserve humility. It should return to the rule of the first monks whose *ora et labora* expressed a proper emphasis and who could show the world rough hands soiled with hard work.

It seems to me that at meal times the religious should ask

himself, like any other man: 'Have I earned this bread? or am I living off other people's work – or worse, off the alms of the poor?' Things would certainly change then, and the world would learn from us the value of work and its importance in the economy of salvation.

Manual work, of course, as it is commonly understood, is not the only way of raising a sweat. When I returned to Europe from the Sahara, I found two young couples in Paris who had decided to work in the Sahara: a doctor and a social worker, a teacher and a nurse.

Instead of working in Paris they had decided to work together in Third World countries. They will undoubtedly 'sweat' more than in France, but it is equally certain that their Christian way of life will be a lot easier and happier.

People are already worrying about the time, now not far off, when our mechanical civilization can offer everyone not just one day off a week but two or even three. What shall we do with so much free time?

Congress follows congress, and apocalyptic voices are raised in warning as if we had reached the world's end – when not knowing what to do men will go mad or at least collapse into a state of nervous exhaustion. I hope only that amongst the multitudes of pagans who add to their cars a private yacht or plane there will still be some Christians capable of occupying their spare time in working for others. Nothing to do? Then I suggest you take a look at the outskirts of our cities.

That is where the refuse of life's great sea ends up, even in our prosperous consumer states. It is difficult to know where to begin, there is so much to be done, so many wounds to soothe.

Where do ex-prisoners go? How do ex-prostitutes live? Where are the rivers of subnormal people hidden? Have you ever visited mental hospitals, old folks' homes?

Have you never gone into the slums? Or into deserted country hamlets where only the old peasants are left, most of them incapable of work in the fields? Time on your hands?

Have you never thought, out of love for Christ, of spending a day – just a day – with an old peasant to help him cut his corn on the hillside because he cannot afford a mechanical mower? Time on your hands?

Has it never occurred to you to spend a day in the dirtiest house in some village helping the poor woman get a bit straight and giving her a chance to catch her breath?

What is that in comparison with the ocean of evils washing over humanity? Nothing, practically nothing. But it is an act of love like Jesus's death on Calvary, and an act of love can achieve a lot. If nothing else, it can give you a bit of true peace and the world the impression that hope is still possible.

Not much?

I think it is.

Chapter Thirteen

LOVE EVERY CREATURE

Bless Yahweh, my soul.
Yahweh my God, how great you are!
Clothed in majesty and glory,
wrapped in a robe of light!

You stretch the heavens out like a tent,
you build your palace on the waters above;
using the clouds as your chariot,
you advance on the wings of the wind;
you use the winds as messengers
and fiery flames as servants.

You fixed the earth on its foundations,
unshakeable for ever and ever;
you wrapped it with the deep as with a robe,
the waters overtopping the mountains.

At your reproof the waters took to flight,
they fled at the sound of your thunder,
cascading over the mountains, into the valleys,
down to the reservoir you made for them;
you imposed the limits they must never cross again,
or they would once more flood the land.

You set springs gushing in ravines,
running down between the mountains,

supplying water for wild animals,
attracting the thirsty wild donkeys;
near there the birds of the air make their nests
and sing among the branches.

From your palace you water the uplands
until the ground has had all that your heavens have to offer;
you make fresh grass grow for cattle,
and those plants made use of by man,
for them to get food from the soil:
wine to make them cheerful,
oil to make them happy
and bread to make them strong.

(Ps 104:1–15)

This psalm is the poem of creation and one of the most beautiful poems. We should sing it often and add so many other verses of our own: what our eyes have discovered, what our love has fixed on. The poem should never end.

If only our hearts were always tender and our souls fresh when we look at creation! What a source of joy it would be on our pilgrimage!

We can pass by and see, or we can pass by and not see: it depends on us.

Creation is like a message written on things, a story told in symbol, a source of conversation for our souls.

But we have to learn how to read, listen and converse.

We are in constant danger of our hearts turning to stone, either with old age or with the petrifaction of sin: and then it is goodbye to our hymn, goodbye to our conversation!

We become the deaf mutes of the Gospel, and in that case only Jesus can cure us.

Loving nature, conversing with nature, is not something extraneous to our love for God: it is a part of it, an essential ingredient.

God speaks to us, teaches us, gives us His first revelation, in the symbols of the created world. Later we shall receive the revelation in word and later still a direct, personal revelation from God, but things still continue to reveal God, as God Himself intended, and we cannot forget it.

Not to look at nature, not to love it to the full, is to refuse to read a document God has specifically composed for us in His love.

St Francis thoroughly understood this truth and made it his own, very particularly his own, and he managed to write that masterpiece of love, the *Canticle of Creatures*: 'My Lord be blessed for all His creatures.'

There is more, however, much more, and it is perhaps our own time which is discovering it. The universe is not only a means whereby God reveals Himself to us, a sort of document in which the Creator explains things to man, but a reality which contains Him. I can even say that it is a kind of Host concealing God Himself under a mysterious veil.

God is *immanent* in His creatures, He is *immense*, He is everywhere. I used to think this was only a catechism answer.

But now I feel it for myself, much more deeply, much more intensely.

God is in nature, God is in matter: matter is divinized, vivified, by God's presence. Now that I know these things I no longer kick stones about as I used to as a child; I have a greater understanding of the Orientals who wish never to do violence to nature because they respect it too much as mediating God's presence.

Perhaps the medievals' love of and attachment to the divine Transcendence has helped us forget that God is also immanent, that He is everywhere. It has created in the past a western religious concept which takes little or no account of natural realities, sees no connection between God and plants, between God and the animals around us.

I shall never forget a group of schoolboys waiting at a station in May sunshine throwing stones at the lizards and throwing the lizards with a laugh on the fire. Such things are relics of a time when a supposed love of God saw no connection with a love of nature and created people, even religious, who saw nothing wrong with hunting, and by that I mean not catching a hare or pheasant for the family to eat, but the brutal joy of seeing game twitch under the shower of lead.

These times have gone, but they are still a very recent thing. And here, if the reader will allow me, I should like to say something about a great prophet of our time and his message to the modern world: Teilhard de Chardin.

This priest, this Jesuit, this scholar was years ahead of his time and did much to force us Christians to resume our dialogue with the cosmos in its physical and metaphysical reality.

It is difficult to limit oneself when talking about him, so versatile and impressive is his thought. The Church is right to say that he must be read with caution and prudence and that some points in his grandiose vision of things are imprecise and vague.

I personally should not choose him as my professor of theology, but I feel that his role – which will pass because he worked alone in such a vast area that future generations will easily go far beyond him – is still of value to us in our change-over from our usual vision of an almost Mediterranean God to God the Creator, Ruler and Soul of the Universe.

Teilhard has helped us rediscover almost physically the presence of God in matter and evolution. Do not tell me he is a pantheist because he sees God in rocks and atoms. His whole life as a priest and a Christian, with its obedience to his vocation and the Church, is there to show us how totally he believed in the Transcendence of God, the Incarnation of the Word, the tragedy of sin and death.

No, like Francis, Teilhard celebrates the Cosmos in song in its new modern dimensions, and I am not afraid of exaggerating when I say that his *Hymn to the Universe* matches the height and depth of the *Canticle of Creatures* and has the same mystical impact. It comes from our own time, and a student of engineering or chemistry will perhaps make it his own with greater joy and not forget it so easily.

It reads like this.

'You are blessed, naked Matter, dry earth, hard rock, you who yield only to violence and oblige us to work if we wish to procure our bread.

You are blessed, dangerous Matter, terrible mother, you who swallow us if we do not chain you.

You are blessed, universal Matter, unlimited duration, bankless river, triple abyss of stars, atoms and generations, you who in breaking down our narrow scale of measurement reveal the very dimensions of God.

You are blessed, impenetrable Matter, stretched everywhere between our souls and the world of absences, you make us long to pierce the seamless veil of phenomena.

You are blessed, immortal Matter, you who one day in dissolving in us will necessarily bring us to the very heart of what is. Without you, without your attacks, without your jerks, we should live inert, puerile, ignorant of ourselves and God.

You who wound and heal, you who bend and restore, you who destroy and build, you who fetter and liberate, lymph of our souls, hand of God, flesh of Christ, Matter I bless you.

Matter I bless and greet you not as the pontiffs of science or the preachers of virtue describe or rather disfigure you, a complex of brutal forces and base appetites, but as you appear to me today in all your truth.

I greet you, inexhaustible capacity for being and becoming.

I greet you, universal power for coupling and union through which the multitude of monads pass in their convergence on the path of the Spirit.

I greet you, harmonious spring of souls, limpid crystal from which the New Jerusalem will be cut.

I greet you, 'divine milieu' full of creative power, agitated ocean of the Spirit, clay kneaded and vivified by the Incarnate Word.

In the belief that they are obeying your irresistible call, men often throw themselves out of love for you into the external abyss of selfish pleasure; they are deceived by a reflection.

To seize you, Matter, starting from a universal contact with everything that moves we must gradually feel the various particular forms of what we hold crumble in our hands until we stand firm grasping what is consistent and unified.

If we wish to possess you we must sublimate you in suffering, having joyfully embraced you.

You reign, Matter, in the serene heights where saints think they can avoid you – flesh so transparent and mobile that we cannot distinguish you any more from the Spirit.

Take me up there, Matter, for strain, separation and death, take me where I can at last chastely embrace the Universe.'

Chapter Fourteen

YOU SHALL NOT MAKE YOURSELF
A CARVED IMAGE

The reader of the Bible is impressed by its insistence on the dangers of idolatry and the vehemence with which this sin is attacked.

The thinking developed by the People of God on their journey through the desert is like a symphonic treatment of the theme of Yahweh's spiritual and transcendent nature.

Moses told the people: 'Yahweh spoke to you from the midst of the fire; you heard the sound of words but saw no shape' (Dt 4:12).

'Take great care what you do, therefore: since you saw no shape on that day at Horeb when Yahweh spoke to you from the midst of the fire, see that you do not act perversely, making yourselves a carved image in the shape of anything at all: whether it be in the likeness of man or of woman, or of any beast on the earth, or of any bird that flies in the heavens, or of any reptile that crawls on the ground, or of any fish in the waters under the earth. When you raise your eyes to heaven, when you see the sun, the moon, the stars, all the array of heaven, do not be tempted to worship them and serve them. Yahweh your God has allotted them to all the peoples under heaven, but as for you, Yahweh has taken you, and brought you out from the furnace of iron, from Egypt, to be a people all his own, as you still are today.

Yahweh has been angry with me on your account; he has

sworn that I shall not cross the Jordan or enter the prosperous land which Yahweh your God is giving you as your heritage. Yes, I am to die in this country; I shall not go across this Jordan; you will go over and take possession of that rich land. Take care therefore not to forget the covenant which Yahweh your God has made with you, by making a carved image of anything that Yahweh your God has forbidden you.'

(Dt 4:15–23)

Yes, the idea and belief of God's transcendence are at the root of all biblical thinking, and it is understandable that the legislator should take precautions to prevent the people from turning God into something material.

'I am Yahweh your God who brought you out of the land of Egypt, out of the house of slavery.

You shall have no gods except me.

You shall not make yourself a carved image or any likeness of anything in heaven or on earth beneath or in the waters under the earth; you shall not bow down to them or serve them. For I, Yahweh your God, am a jealous God and I punish the father's fault in the sons, the grandsons and the great-grandsons of those who hate me; but I show kindness to thousands of those who love me and keep my commandments.'

(Ex 20:2–6)

I have often wondered where the danger of idolatry comes from.

Is it in us or outside us? Does it affect the ancient Hebrews or also us moderns who claim to have put the ancient attitudes behind us? I have come to the conclusion that the danger is in us and that the sin of idolatry affects all ages. The people of the Old Testament were tempted to make idols of wood, ivory or silver to hang from their camels' saddles, while the people of the New Testament carry saints' medals in their pockets instead of God in their hearts.

The motive is more or less the same. We are too idle to make the effort to think of God as beyond time and space, in His Transcendence and Mystery – it is so much more convenient to give Him a cheap face in order to replace His remoteness with something tangible, something close to us, something above all which will heal us when we are ill, enrich us when we are poor.

Now I must make it quite clear that I am not criticizing devotion to the saints. Devotion to the saints is commendable when it is properly integrated into one's central worship: the adoration of God.

No, I am talking about belief not in a witness of the Church triumphant but in pieces of wood with supposedly magic powers, all too frequent in the undergrowth of post-Christian piety.

Originally the articles were Christian objects which served a useful purpose, but in the hands of idolaters they have become idols, idols in the form of medals, holy pictures and crucifixes. In my view the more a people's faith declines – real, strong, enlightened, virile faith – the more piety-stalls proliferate; the more superficial piety becomes and the more it approximates to a fear of becoming ill or the hope of winning the pools, the greater need man feels to build altars to his own idols.

I have found these altars of modern idolatry everywhere, even in church. Imagine what it must be like outside!

I remember a self-styled atheist who could not end his day without a sign of the cross.

I have met many lorry-drivers in the Sahara who live as if God did not take care of them and who have pictures of St Rita or St Anthony as charms on their windscreens!

That is idolatry.

This is not to say that the question is an easy one. What is ever clear in the muddled human heart? What significance are we to attribute, for example, to a cross round somebody's neck?

Is it a reminder of his parents' faith or a kind of totem or charm? One can never tell. Who is to say that it has no mysterious and hidden power of protection? Idolatry and superstition are still religious forms, certainly, however unsophisticated, and they frequently occur in people who have lost the true faith – the dying ashes of a lost inheritance.

The Bible is really biting, however, when it tries to convince people that an idol is an idol, a thing of no value, a god who neither sees, feels nor moves, a god who is powerless to help.

Jeremiah says in his celebrated letter to Baruch on idolatry:

Plated with gold and silver, their tongues polished smooth by a craftsman, they are counterfeit and have no power to speak. As though for a girl fond of finery, these pagans take gold and make crowns for the heads of their gods. Sometimes, the priests actually filch gold and silver from their gods to spend themselves, even using it on presents for the temple prostitutes. They dress up these gods of silver, gold and wood, in clothes, like human beings, although they cannot protect themselves either from tarnish or woodworm, in spite of the purple cloaks they drape them in. Their faces even have to be dusted, owing to the dust of the temple which settles thick on them. One holds a sceptre like the governor of a province, yet is powerless to put anyone who offends him to death; another holds sword and axe in his right hand, yet is powerless to defend himself against war or thieves. From this it is evident that they are not gods; do not be afraid of them.

However much was paid for them, there is still no breath of life in them. Being unable to walk, they have to be carried on men's shoulders, which shows how futile they are. It is humiliating for their worshippers too, who have to stand them up again if they fall over. Once they have been stood up, they cannot move on their own; if they tilt askew, they cannot right themselves; offerings made to them might as well be made to dead men. Whatever is sacrificed to them, the priests re-sell and pocket the profit; while their wives salt down part of it, but give nothing to the poor or to the helpless. As to the sacrifices themselves, why, women during their periods and women in childbed are not afraid to touch them! As you can see from these examples that they are not gods, do not be afraid of them.

(Ba 6:7–14, 24–8)

People have been tempted since time immemorial to ascribe magic power to things and places. To the Samaritan woman at the well trying to defend herself by engaging him in a religious dispute, Jesus uttered that magnificent phrase: 'The hour has come when true worshippers will worship the Father in spirit and truth' (Jn 4:23).

Worshipping God 'in spirit and truth' is the way to purify the soul of the tendency to adore idols, to protect it from the constant danger of worshipping human values, of believing in what is perishable, of according excessive importance to power and riches. 'True worshippers worship the Father in spirit and truth.' That is how we can escape the tangled undergrowth of spiritist magic, the confusing fog of mysterious beliefs, faith in amulets, powers ascribed to bits of wood . . . and holy water.

Do not be scandalized. In some places where faith in Christ is no more than a memory and sacramental life has disappeared, I have seen people put great value on the annual blessing of the house. Their idea seems to be that the water is something magic, a panacea against illness, a means of driving out evil spirits and powers. Young people increasingly react against this type of piety and, so they say, prefer atheism. I am not at all sure they really understand the problem.

A high proportion of what the young call atheism is probably only the need to be free of this fog of superstition and

93

to rid themselves of a traditional piety they no longer find convincing.

Many young people are casting down the idols of the past and rebelling against a way of thinking about God which offends their modern cultural sensibilities.

The moderns may have many faults, but at least they have the merit of wanting to understand. And given that the house inherited from their grandmothers is awash with a piety based on oleographs in bad taste, they prefer to consign the lot to the cellar and leave the walls of their soul bare and uncluttered.

Bare walls?

Would to God this were true! It would be the finest preparation for the future religious development of their souls.

But . . . when the picture of St Anthony and the oleograph of the Holy Family have been removed, they are soon replaced by photos of idolized football teams and then a long series of modern idols: cinema stars, dancers, pop singers, guitarists.

Alas! Idolatry begins on another level because the soul, this poor soul deprived of its God, cannot do without Him and so looks for substitutes, even fourth rate ones. But at least these do not perform miracles, and that says something for their manufacturers!

And what about people too old to play soccer and jive, who are scandalized at the frivolity of youth's idols and tell them so?

What do they put in place of St Joseph when they have thrown his picture away?

The autographed photo of some influential VIP; letters of recommendation; people who can offer promotion, career opportunities, transfers long dreamed of.

Candles are lit as our grandparents lit them in church – but now they are candles of adulation, and the incense is flattery.

And let us not talk of the tricks resorted to to reach these idols, the acts of prostitution to receive their favours: they would be worthy of the cleverest harlequin.

PART III

Apart from the family and work as schools created by God for our training in His eternal love, there is another essential human-divine activity as continuous as breathing and the beating of the heart: prayer.

Prayer, from childlike invocation to infused contemplation, accompanies the development of the soul in its increasing maturity and guides it to the peak of union with God. This is the subject of the following seven meditations.

Chapter Fifteen

PRAISE OF GOD

When the soul opens itself to the love of God, the first word it utters is a word of praise, a cry of exultation.

> I love Yahweh, my strength,
> my stronghold and my refuge.
>
> (Ps 18:1–2)

It is like a need bottled up in our inmost heart which at last finds an outlet:

> My heart is ready, God
> – I mean to sing and play.
>   Awake, my muse,
> awake, lyre and harp,
>   I mean to wake the Dawn!
>
> (Ps 108:1–2)

It is like a spring which travels miles underground and then finally gushes out in a silver stream:

> God, you are my God, I am seeking you,
> my soul is thirsting for you,
> my flesh is longing for you,
> a land parched, weary and waterless.
>
> (Ps 63:1–2)

Prayer is above all a reply. Later it will include requests, many of them, but basically it is a reply.

This is because God makes the first request.

If He did not speak first, all our talking would be in vain.

If He did not leave His isolation, nobody could liberate us from ours; if He did not call to us from the abysses of being, nobody would dream of replying. Yes, to have love you need two people, and man is the passive partner in love.

God is the first, the active partner.

Jesus said:

> 'No one can come to me
> unless he is drawn by the Father who sent me.'
>
> (Jn 6:44)

It is the Father who takes the initiative. He comes to us from the silence of His Transcendence and calls us by name.

And man replies.

That is how the conversation of prayer begins.

When we become aware that He is calling us, when we hear resounding in the emptiness of our poverty the deep echo of the petition He Himself has placed in our being, we are disposed to prayer, we have placed ourselves in a position in which prayer is possible.

And as we said earlier, the first reply is a 'thank you'.

It could not be otherwise. We are creatures by nature, He the Creator.

Unless we establish ourselves in that particular relationship, we are not living in truth and we cannot pray.

As he discovers his creatureliness, man says to his Creator:

Lord, you have been
our refuge age after age.

Before the mountains were born,
before the earth or the world came to birth,
you were God from all eternity and for ever.

You can turn man back into dust
by saying, 'Back to what you were, you sons of men!'
To you, a thousand years are a single day,
a yesterday now over, an hour of the night.

(Ps 90:1–4)

And again:

> Come, let us praise Yahweh joyfully,
> acclaiming the Rock of our safety;
> let us come into his presence with thanksgiving,
> acclaiming him with music.

> For Yahweh is a great God,
> a greater King than all other gods;
> from depths of earth to mountain top
> everything comes under his rule;
> the sea belongs to him, he made it,
> so does the land, he shaped this too.

(Ps 95:1–5)

This is our response to God's call.

To any gift however great or small the creature who opens his eyes and heart to life responds with praise.

It must be so.

To gasp with wonder at the beauty of a sunset and to shout with joy at the sight of a new-born child is to pray, and our prayer is a gasp of admiration.

> Yahweh, our Lord,
> how great your name throughout the earth!

> Above the heavens is your majesty chanted
> by the mouths of children, babes in arms.

(Ps 8:1–2)

Yes, how true that is: God's majesty is chanted 'by the mouths of children'.

We must be children if we wish to pray, or at least become children.

The great of this world are too sceptical, too 'experienced', too 'clever'; they remain in their silence, closed to the prayer of adoration.

But if we are small by nature or have become small by grace we can offer praise and sing in ecstasy:

I look up at your heavens, made by your fingers,
at the moon and stars you set in place –
ah, what is man that you should spare a thought for
  him,
the son of man that you should care for him?

Yet you have made him little less than a god,
you have crowned him with glory and splendour,
made him lord over the work of your hands,
set all things under his feet,

sheep and oxen, all these,
yes, wild animals too,
birds in the air, fish in the sea
travelling the paths of the ocean.

(Ps 8:3–8)

Now this is quite something! But only the small man discovers he is big, king of creation, 'little less than a god'. The 'great', the 'wise', the 'powerful' cannot see or understand – or sing. They do not pray, and this is the severest possible defect, the most wretched state to which a man can sink.

How vital it is to become small if we wish to learn how to pray!

How vital it is to feel insignificant if we wish to say:

Send out your light and your truth,
  let these be my guide,
to lead me to your holy mountain
  and to the place where you live.

Then I shall go to the altar of God,
  to the God of my joy.

(Ps 43: 3–4a)

to respect the truth of humility if we wish to pray:

Blessed be Yahweh, my rock,
who trains my hands for war
and my fingers for battle,
my love, my bastion,
my citadel, my saviour,
I shelter behind him, my shield.

(Ps 144:1–2)

Yes, humility is truth, and truth is humility.

It is true that man is 'little less than a god', but we must be little to understand it. It is true that God is our God and that everything we have comes from Him, but how hard it is to understand for someone who is not spiritually a child! Our Lady understood it, and she put it into words in a prayer that is and will always be the pattern of every prayer of adoration, the perfect response to all God's requests:

'My soul proclaims the greatness of the Lord
and my spirit exults in God my saviour;
because he has looked upon his lowly handmaid.
Yes, from this day forward all generations will call
                    me blessed,
for the Almighty has done great things for me.
Holy is his name,
and his mercy reaches from age to age for those
                    who fear him.

He has shown the power of his arm,
he has routed the proud of heart.
He has pulled down princes from their thrones and
exalted the lowly.
The hungry he has filled with good things, the rich
sent empty away.
He has come to the help of Israel his servant,
mindful of his mercy
– according to the promise he made to our
ancestors –
of his mercy to Abraham and to his descendents
for ever.'

(Lk 1:46–55)

It was her answer to God's eternal request for the Incarnation of His Son.

Chapter Sixteen

PETITION

Prayer is not only a reply but frequently – very frequently – a petition.

> Take pity on me, God, take pity on me.
> I call on God the Most High,
> on God who has done everything for me.
>
> (Ps 57:1–2)

One does not have to go very far in life to learn to call, shout, beseech. How fragile and weak and little man is on earth! How brittle his stability, which the merest trifle can upset.

> Save me, God! The water
>   is already up to my neck!
>
> I am sinking in the deepest swamp,
>   there is no foothold;
> I have stepped into deep water
>   and the waves are washing over me.
>
> (Ps 69:1–2)

This is how the prayer of petition arises, a prayer so great and all-pervading that for many people it is synonymous with prayer. For many people praying means asking, and often they are unaware of other forms of conversing with God.

Worn out with calling, my throat is hoarse,
my eyes are strained, looking for my God.

God, you know how foolish I have been,
my offences are not hidden from you.

(Ps 69:3, 5)

And again:

My soul is all troubled,
my life is on the brink of Sheol.

(Ps 88:3)

From the depths I call to you, Yahweh,
Lord, listen to my cry for help!
Listen compassionately
    to my pleading!

If you never overlooked our sins, Yahweh,
Lord, could anyone survive?

(Ps 130:1–3)

Sometimes when our distress is exceptionally intense, we feel that God Himself is against us:

Pity me, Yahweh, I have no strength left,
heal me, my bones are in torment,
my soul is in utter torment.
Yahweh, how long will you be?

(Ps 6:2–3)

Your own hands shaped me, modelled me;
    and would you now have second thoughts and
                                destroy me?

(Jb 10:8)

You have plunged me to the bottom of the Pit,
to its darkest, deepest place,
weighted down by your anger,
drowned beneath your waves.

(Ps 88:6–7)

The fact is that the person now has a deeper awareness of sin, and his relationship with God has consequently been radically upset.

To the person who really loves, sin is the betrayal of a friend, infidelity to a spouse, the desertion of a father. And God is this Friend, this Spouse, this Father.

When the soul realizes the horrible thing it has done, it cannot help crying out and weeping for sorrow.

Have mercy on me, O God, in your goodness,
in your great tenderness wipe away my faults;
wash me clean of my guilt,
purify me from my sin.

For I am well aware of my faults,
I have my sin constantly in mind,
having sinned against none other than you,
having done what you regard as wrong.

You are just when you pass sentence on me,
blameless when you give judgement.
You know I was born guilty,
a sinner from the moment of conception.

God, create a clean heart in me,
put into me a new and constant spirit,
do not banish me from your presence,
do not deprive me of your holy spirit.

(Ps 51:1–5, 10–11)

I think this Miserere psalm could be recited every day of our lives and still not be sufficient. And many of us – those who have not managed to reach a state of perfect love in this life – will have to recite it for aeons on end in purgatory.

I do not need to imagine a purgatory of fire; I can think of a place like my cell when I am alone or a dry desert landscape where only God and I are present.

Charity becomes the fire which burns the fibres of the soul. The memory of what our poor life has actually been compared with what it should have been is enough to instil in us the desire for repentance. The sight of our love for God betrayed, derided, despised, sold down the river, prostituted, will plunge the sword of pain to the centre of our being and make us pine with sorrow.

I am memorizing Psalm 88, which I regard as the prayer of purgatory, partly because it contains some phrases which to be true and genuine in myself would need the night of the soul.

> Yahweh my God, I call for help all day,
> I weep to you all night;
> may my prayer reach you
> hear my cries for help;
>
> for my soul is all troubled,
> my life is on the brink of Sheol;
> I am numbered among those who go down to the Pit,
> a man bereft of strength:
>
> a man alone, down among the dead,
> among the slaughtered in their graves,
> among those you have forgotten,
> those deprived of your protecting hand.
>
> You have plunged me to the bottom of the Pit,
> to its darkest, deepest place,
> weighted down by your anger,
> drowned beneath your waves.

You have turned my friends against me
and made me repulsive to them;
in prison and unable to escape,
my eyes are worn out with suffering.

Yahweh, I invoke you all day,
I stretch out my hands to you:
are your marvels meant for the dead,
can ghosts rise up to praise you?

Who talks of your love in the grave,
of your faithfulness in the place of perdition?
Do they hear about your marvels in the dark,
about your righteousness in the land of oblivion?

But I am here, calling for your help,
praying to you every morning:
why do you reject me?
Why do you hide your face from me?

Wretched, slowly dying since my youth,
I bore your terrors – now I am exhausted;
your anger overwhelmed me,
you destroyed me with your terrors
which, like a flood, were round me, all day long,
all together closing in on me.
You have turned my friends and neighbours against me,
now darkness is my one companion left.

(Ps 88)

Purgatory will be like this if I have not learnt to live love to
the full in this life, and when I think of it I am afraid.

In the end who deserves hell, who deserves Heaven? After
all, are our lives any more than systematized mediocrity?

Do we not belong to the army of the lukewarm – those afraid
of going too far?

Was not Christ condemned to death because of people who did not sufficiently care? In the praetorium and on Calvary, was not the crowd, with a few exceptions, a collection of people who 'couldn't really care less'? Was not Jesus condemned in ridicule?

He was in earnest, but were most of the other people there? Were they really interested in Him? Were they not equally ready to shout 'Hosanna' and 'Crucify him'?

Yes, Love was condemned in ridicule, in disinterest, in a what-does-it-matter-to-me attitude, in the golden mediocrity which floods the earth and drowns it in nausea.

This is why saints are few and far between.

Our destiny is therefore purgatory, a long one, where we shall have time to consider that our superficial, distracted, tepid lives were intolerable to Someone who loves as God does.

And we shall see written on the door that phrase from Revelation:

'I wish you were hot or cold, but since you are neither, but only lukewarm, I will spit you out of my mouth.'

(3:15)

Chapter Seventeen

TRUST AS PRAYER

One of the hardest battles in the spiritual life, perhaps I should say the hardest, is the struggle to see God in our trivial human happenings. How often we have to renew our act of faith! At first we are tempted to see only ourselves, to believe only in ourselves, to value only ourselves. Then gradually we perceive that the thread of life has a rationale, a mysterious unity, and we are led to think that we meet God in its basic stages. Then again, as our religious experience grows, we begin to realize that we meet God not only in the big events of our lives but in all the events, however small and apparently insignificant.

God is never absent from our lives, He cannot be, because 'in Him we live, and move, and exist' (Ac 17:28). But it requires so much effort to turn this truth into a habit!

We need repeated acts of faith before we learn to sail with confidence on the 'immense and endless sea' which is God (St Gregory Nazienzen), knowing that if we founder we do so in Him, the divine eternal ever-present God. How fortunate we are if we can learn to navigate our frail craft on this sea and remain serene even when the storm is raging!

> I love you, Yahweh, my strength.
> Yahweh is my rock and my bastion,
> my deliverer is my God.
>
> (Ps 18:1-2)

The waves of death encircled me,
the torrents of Belial burst on me;
the cords of Sheol girdled me,
the snares of death were before me.

In my distress I called to Yahweh
and to my God I cried;
from his Temple he heard my voice,
my cry came to his ears.

Then the earth quivered and quaked,
the foundations of the mountains trembled.

(Ps 18:4–7)

He sends from on high and takes me,
he draws me from deep waters,
he delivers me from my powerful enemy,
from a foe too strong for me.

(Ps 18:16–17)

David experienced this dramatic rescue by God when he advanced against Goliath, his only weapon weakness, his only support the confidence of youth (1 S 17).

How wonderful this scene is, a stripling striking the Philistine giant dead with a pebble! The youth *lives in his God* and knows that his confidence rests on God the Invincible. The impossible becomes possible, Goliath is struck down, and the memory of it will inspire David for the rest of his life.

Yahweh is my shepherd,
  I lack nothing.

In meadows of green grass he lets me lie.
To the waters of repose he leads me;
there he revives my soul.

(Ps 23:1–3a)

He will celebrate his victory in song long after his youth is over, when his life is harsher and faith more difficult.

Yes, the older we grow the more danger there is of outgrowing our childhood. Faith, great faith, needs the atmosphere of spiritual infancy. And if we lose that, faith is endangered, we find it difficult to *trust* God any more. We grow up, we become 'adult', and our reasoning destroys the substance of our proper sense of dependence on God. We must constantly recall Jesus's warning: 'Unless you change and become like little children you will never enter the kingdom of heaven' (Mt 18:3). We must try and remain very small where life forces us to be big.

The spirit moves in the opposite direction to nature, and the greatest achievement in matters of faith is for a grown person to become small, an adult to return to his childhood, a serpent to change into a dove.

And if, when we are old, full of human experience and wisdom, sharpened by the years and 'cunning as serpents', we are also 'harmless as doves' and 'like little children', we shall be able to lift our hearts up to God and sing with David:

> If you live in the shelter of Elyon
> and make your home in the shadow of Shaddai,
> you can say to Yahweh, 'My refuge, my fortress,
> my God in whom I trust!'

> He rescues you from the snares
> of fowlers hoping to destroy you;
> he covers you with his feathers,
> and you find shelter underneath his wings.

> You need not fear for the terrors of night,
> the arrow that flies in the daytime,
> the plague that stalks in the dark,
> the scourge that wreaks havoc in broad daylight.

No disaster can overtake you,
no plague come near your tent:
he will put you in his angels' charge
to guard you wherever you go.

They will support you on their hands
in case you hurt your foot against a stone;
you will tread on lion and adder,
trample on savage lions and dragons.

'I rescue all who cling to me,
I protect whoever knows my name,
I answer everyone who invokes me,
I am with them when they are in trouble;
I bring them safety and honour.
I give them life, long and full,
and show them how I can save.'

(Ps 91:1–6, 10–16)

What a longing this psalm inspires! How it makes me want to live a life totally absorbed at last by confidence in God!

How I should love to remain serene in trials, not to fear the terrors of night and the scourge that wreaks havoc at the noon of life!

This is not easy, and we have a lifetime in which to gain this victory and attain this state of peace. Our task is a hard one, a brick-by-brick construction of our spiritual temple, a step-by-step advance towards total faith which only God can give, via acts of faith which depend on us and on our dedication. As in everything else, God looks for our collaboration. He gives us the boat and the oars but asks us to do the rowing, and the more we row the easier it becomes.

Whether we receive gifts in the future depends on our present commitment, just as the athlete's effectiveness depends on constant training.

David was stronger in faith after accepting Goliath's

challenge, Joshua closer to God after attacking Jericho with nothing but trumpets.

Judith was dearer to God after accepting in faith to enter Holofernes' tent, Joseph a 'juster' man after obeying the angel and taking Mary to be his wife.

Acts of faith accustom us to a life of trust in God; trust generates trust and leads to absolute intimacy, perfect unity.

> Yahweh, my heart has no lofty ambitions,
>> my eyes do not look too high.
> I am not concerned with great affairs
>> or marvels beyond my scope.
> Enough for me to keep my soul tranquil and quiet
>> like a child in its mother's arms,
> as content as a child that has been weaned.
>
> (Ps 131:1–2)

That is the peak of religious life on earth: keeping our soul tranquil and quiet like a child in its mother's arms.

If we wished to sum up the relationship that should exist between man and God, if we wished to give as exact an example as possible of the trust on which the peace of those who live in the mystery of God depends, we could not do better than point to the infant sleeping in the strong arms of its mother, close to the womb of its being, safe under the watchful eye of the person who gave him his existence and who thought of him before he ever was.

Chapter Eighteen

PRAYER AND LIFE

We have all had the experience of going into a sacristy and seeing a good Christian bent over his breviary.

Imagine that it is Friday and that the priest is reciting Lauds, Psalm 143.

> Yahweh, hear my prayer,
> listen to my pleading,
> answer me faithfully, righteously.

He lifts his head as the visitor enters and says, 'Can I help you?'

While waiting for the answer his eye wanders to the next verse:

> Do not put your servant on trial,
> no one is virtuous by your standards.

'I should like to have a mass said, Father.'

> An enemy who hounds me
> to crush me into the dust,
> forces me to dwell in darkness
> like the dead of long ago.

'Would next Friday at eight be OK?'

> My spirit fails me.

'Would you accept this offering please, Father?'

And my heart is full of fear.

'Thank you. Is there anything else?'

I stretch out my hands.

'No, that's all, thank you. Goodbye, Father.'

Like thirsty ground I yearn for you.

This is no joke. All too often we treat prayer like this.

If you are not guilty, thank God, because you have reached a new stage in prayer which is far from easy.

Manzoni was right when he called the human heart a 'jumble'.

And the jumble persists into our most serious activity – talking with God.

How difficult it is to put a bit of order into our minds, to leave the formalism of prayer and turn prayer into something alive, a living union with God!

Too often and for too long prayer and life meet like strangers on the road, live like neighbours not on speaking terms, relate like a mother-in-law and daughter-in-law, grow away from each other like a couple who are no longer in love and who stay together only because they have not the courage to separate.

And that is not the worst of it. Prayer and life can sometimes coexist like two criminals in the same cell or even like two corpses in the same tomb.

How good we are!

And so used to deluding ourselves! Do we never hear mass with hatred for our brother in our hearts?

Could we never bring ourselves to withold mass offerings?

Everything is possible when we leave the straight and narrow.

And when God is tired of our duplicity, He will say such terrible things as Jeremiah or even more Malachi record:

> I will send the curse on you and curse your very blessing. Indeed I have already cursed it, since there is not a single one of you who takes this to heart. Now watch how I am going to paralyse your arm and throw dung in your face – the dung from your very solemnities – and sweep you away with it.
>
> (Ml 2:2b–4)

However, that is not what I wished to talk about – it is too obvious.

I wished to talk about the difficulty of balancing prayer and life even when we are on the right road.

I wished to stress one particular thing: our devotional exercises should not encumber an already overloaded day; the inner spirit must not be stifled by the interminable formulas and actions of a piety which no longer speaks to the heart or mind; action must not eliminate contemplation; contemplation incorrectly understood must not make us eccentric, ill-tempered, disagreeable.

We may begin with a very clear and simple remark. If I find I cannot say the Office because charity makes too many demands on my time, either I ask my superior to dispense me or I dispense myself. Saying the breviary during mass or when I am cooking is not taking it seriously at all. If I do that I am regarding prayer as no more than a *juridical obligation*, a sort of toll to be paid as a price for living. If I say the Office at all, it must be done properly, in peace and quiet, in such a way that it benefits me, nourishes my devotional life in an intelligent and balanced way; above all it must not be a burden.

In the pre-conciliar Church it was not at all unusual to hear a priest intoning his *Iam lucis orto sidere* at eleven o'clock at night. This type of thing possibly helped to develop man's sense of duty, but it definitely created a misunderstanding of prayer as life. The Council, fortunately, made a clean sweep, and even though we shall need patience and courage in applying its spirit and letter, the new times will help to put behind us a type of formalism which to my mind seriously threatened Christianity.

Age quod agis should apply not only to all our human activities in general but to the most serious business of the day, the most radical effort of life, in particular: prayer. Prayer must become a living reality if I am not to complicate still further with external acts an already complicated interior life.

If I wish to attend mass properly on a Sunday, I must make every effort to enter into things. If I wish to get the best out of the liturgical readings, I should close my prayer-book and listen attentively.

If I wish to meditate, I must go somewhere where I can have complete silence. And above all I should not go to a second mass with the idea of taking out a higher heavenly insurance, as many pious – and muddled – people seem to.

And so on.

There is something else, however, which is even more important if we are to eliminate or at least reduce the elements within ourselves which militate against the 'wholeness', the strong, vital integrity, of our lives.

We must eliminate or at least reduce the tensions between action and contemplation, apostolate and prayer, external and internal activity, dedication to others and dedication to self. How can we do this?

People say: 'I'm too busy with work at the moment to find time for prayer.' Or: 'How can I pray with five children to look after?' Or: 'When can I pray with eight hours' office-work and then the housework to do?'

These arguments betray a very serious shortcoming: they radically underestimate the value of human activity.

The impression they give is that professional, social and

family life is totally separate from prayer and the life of the soul.

The advice of pious people serves merely to aggravate the confusion and the depreciation of human activities.

These people say: 'In the morning offer up your day's work and it becomes a prayer', or 'Every so often raise up your heart in prayer', etc.

They talk as if we cannot be united to God unless we leave our work, as if to be a Christian means putting our duties aside!

This betrays a sad confusion and is the product of an age with no proper theology of the laity.

Furthermore it is based on a 'disincarnate' piety, more angelic than human.

Work, study, the household jobs, looking after the children are all such important things!

They are also holy things, because they are human values willed by God to whom I have to devote myself totally in thought and deed.

My work is no easier for making a sign of the cross over it, my day no lighter for offering it up in the morning prayer. On the contrary! But the first thing I must understand and believe is *that my work is of enormous value, that the duties incumbent on me as a human being are holy because they are willed by God and I fulfil them in obedience to His Law*.

And if God allows me a little free time after all the work and chores, I can devote a few minutes to contemplation, enabling my life to achieve its proper balance.

People say: 'I've got too much on in my apostolate, I can't pray.'

Now the contradiction here is so obvious that only Manzoni's word is adequate: our poor hearts are nothing but a 'jumble'.

How can there be any opposition between two ways of expressing love for the same Person?

If prayer is love for God, how can it be excluded from another form of love for God, the apostolate?

Surely the first commandment cannot be said to contradict the second, which 'resembles it' (Mt 22:39)?

How can the charity which takes us out towards our neighbour not take us out towards God at the same time?

Unless, of course, what we call 'apostolate' is not love for our neighbour but agitation, activism, self-seeking, escapism – the 'heresy of action', as the Abbé Chautard called it.

In that case we should have to say not: 'I've got too much on in my apostolate, I can't pray', but: 'I am deluding myself by doing what we call apostolic work, whereas in fact I'm simply wasting my time seeking myself in contact with my neighbour and I've no time to spend with God.'

God is too simple in His relations with us, and He cannot continually thwart us when we are trying to find Him.

But . . . we must really wish to find Him, and this basic desire will unify all our various actions.

We must want to go to Him, to find Him, to look for His will and love; to go to Him with all our being as it left His creative hand and as it has been damaged by our sins.

We must want to go to Him with our spirits and bodies, with our daily effort and the graces we have been given, with our brothers who are with us in the struggle and with the aspirations of the entire universe. Two things are certain in this 'going to God'. The first is that in cases of conflict or doubt charity must be considered the supreme rule, and the second is that as long as we are on earth the bond uniting us with God is the desire to achieve union with Him, and however imperfect that desire it remains the fundamental and vital basis of our religious life.

Chapter Nineteen

PRAYER AS SACRIFICE

It has been said that there are peoples without cities, cities without walls, men without art, but no people, city or men without sacrifice. Sacrifice as a form of prayer, as an expression of religious devotion, was born with man and will die with man.

From the primitive forms found among animists to the organized forms of Hebrewism, from the sacrificed ram of every good Muslim to the sacrifices of the Hindus and Shintoists in the east, sacrifice has shown itself to be a universal form of prayer. If ever we arrived on another planet and there were intelligent beings there, I wager we should find them constructing an altar and sacrificing a victim.

The essential elements of sacrifice – an assembly, an altar, a priest, a victim – are as basic to us as heart, blood and lungs. Urged on by the irrepressible need to express his love for God with presents, man on earth has expressed his subjection to God by offering on altars gifts from his flocks, first-fruits from his harvests.

The Bible offers the most complete and developed casuistry of sacrifice, and one has only to read Leviticus to see this.

'If your offering is a holocaust of an animal out of the herd . . . if your offering is an animal out of the flock . . . if your offering is a holocaust of a bird . . . when you are going to offer an oblation of dough baked in the oven . . .'

If one had to depict in art the essence of religious forms of the ancients, one would unhesitatingly paint a congregation round an altar at the moment when one of them – the priest – was offering sacrifice.

Why the victim, however? Why blood? Why was it not enough to offer peace-offerings as they did at harvest-time?

Peoples universally expressed their subjection to the Creator by offering corn or honey or wool or a candle, and they universally included blood as an element of sacrifice.

Why?

Man felt that something had been snapped, that the balance of things was upset, that peace-offerings were adequate at certain moments but inadequate at others when something more was needed to express one's state of soul. Theologians talk about original sin, St Augustine talked about a disorder. The fact is that man had realized his sinfulness and recognized increasingly that he had to pay, and that blood was the proper price for sin. This thirst for a victim, this urgent need to shed blood and bridge the gap created by sin between God and man is characteristic of world religion.

Humanity seems to be saying, 'Lord, we are nothing but riff-raff, we have done violence, we have killed, robbed, betrayed. We do not deserve your pardon . . . But look at this innocent victim dying on the altar and pardon us by its blood.' Ancient peoples even went so far – totally contrary to God's wishes – as to sacrifice babies and innocent young girls.

They seemed to want to force the hand of justice: O God, look at this! The Hebrews sacrificed millions of victims; rivers of blood were spilt to satisfy the immense thirst for justice in sinful man. When the Temple was inaugurated in Jerusalem, Solomon offered Yahweh 22,000 oxen and 120,000 sheep (1 K 8:62) – a sign of the religious sentiments of ancient peoples.

The most typical summary of the past, however, the finest synthesis of the concept of sacrifice which was to remain as an image and symbol of 'what was to come' was undoubtedly the passover.

'Each man must take an animal from the flock, one for each family, and slaughter it between the two evenings. Some of the blood must then be put on the two doorposts and the lintel of the houses where it is eaten. That night the flesh is to be eaten, roasted over the fire. You shall eat it like this: with a girdle round your waist, sandals on your feet, a staff in your hand. It is a passover in honour of Yahweh!

(Ex 12:3–11)

And so they did.

And in memory of that 'passover' the Hebrews celebrated the Pasch annually by sacrificing a lamb. It was the ultimate symbol, from our point of view completely luminous, of what was to happen later: the real, definitive and radical 'passover', *the Pasch of the New Alliance*.

Naturally none of the sacrifices of ancient peoples was anything but symbolic – symbolic of a reality yet to come, of a history yet to mature. That history would be inaugurated by Jesus, the Christ. As a Hebrew and son of His people, He would eat the passover every year with bitter herbs and His loins girt, in memory of the flight from Egypt and the crossing of the Reed Sea.

He would do so with Mary and Joseph as a child, with other relatives and friends during the rest of His short thirty-three years, and with His twelve disciples for that last time in the upper room in Jerusalem.

On that occasion, St Luke tells us, Jesus had told His disciples: 'I have longed to eat this passover with you before I suffer' (22:15).

No longer, however, was it the old passover: the symbol was at an end, the reality of the only authentic sacrifice was about to enter the stage of history.

As they were eating, Jesus took some bread, and when he had said the blessing he broke it and gave it to his disciples.

'Take it and eat;' he said 'this is my body.' Then he took a cup, and when he had returned thanks he gave it to them. 'Drink all of you from this,' he said 'for this is my blood, the blood of the covenant, which is to be poured out for many for the forgiveness of sins.'

(Mt 26:26–8)

Jesus was to offer himself as innocent victim to the Father on the altar of the world, with all humanity round him, pay the price for all and thus bring the past to a definitive close. That sacrifice, the offertory of which was the Last Supper, which was brought to completion the following day on Calvary and which is repeated at every mass throughout history, was to be the once-for-all, universally valid sacrifice of which the ancient sacrifices were symbols and future masses 'memorials'.

In an eternal present, Jesus, who had accepted in the Incarnation solidarity with all mankind, assumed the role of Eternal Priest and offered Himself as a bloody victim on Calvary, the altar of the world. This sacrifice – foreshadowed in the passover of the old law as a remembrance of the journey from slavery in Egypt to the freedom of the Promised Land, transformed into a reality in the oblation of the Lamb of God at the Last Supper and on Calvary, approved by the Father at Jesus's Resurrection and Ascension into Heaven, and renewed at each mass to the end of time in the strength and will of Christ who foresaw and willed all consecrations when He said, 'Do this as a memorial of me' – is the unique and eternal sacrifice acceptable to God.

No hymn, no poem, expresses this so well as the *Exsultet* of Holy Saturday.

'This is the paschal feast wherein is slain the true Lamb whose blood hallows the doorposts of the faithful. This is the night when, long ago, thou didst cause our forefathers, the sons of Israel, in their passage out of Egypt, to pass dryshod

123

over the Red Sea. This is the night which swept away the blackness of sin by the light of the fiery pillar. This is the night which at this hour throughout the world restores to grace and yokes to holiness those who believe in Christ, detaching them from worldly vice and all the murk of sin. On this night Christ burst the bonds of death and rose victorious from the grave. What good would life have been to us without redemption? How wonderful the pity and care thou hast shown us; how far beyond all reckoning thy loving-kindness! To ransom thy slave, thou gavest up thy Son! O truly necessary sin of Adam, that Christ's death blotted out; and happy fault, that merited so great a Redeemer! Blessed indeed is this, the sole night counted worthy to mark the season and the hour in which Christ rose again from the grave. It is this night of which the scripture says: And the night shall be bright as day. Such is my joy that night itself is light! So holy, this night, it banishes all crimes, washes guilt away, restores lost innocence, brings mourners joy.'

Jesus's offering at the Last Supper (the new passover), the completion of His sacrifice on Calvary and His Resurrection (the Father's reply to the Son's love) form an inseparable whole: the reality of Christianity, the New Covenant, the dawn of the new creation, the centre of the religious universe, the ineffable synthesis of our faith, hope and charity.

When we join with the community of believers at Holy Mass, we are celebrating the Lord's death and Resurrection until He comes again.

The liturgical assembly of the Mass is *the* religious act, the living memorial of Easter, which enables us to accomplish the same 'passover' from death to life, from sin to grace.

When Christ comes to us in the Eucharist and bathes us in His blood, we enter the fulness of God, we come under the Father's forgiving gaze, we are touched by the Spirit's love, and the vital principle of our bodily and spiritual resurrection is instilled into us.

Taking part in the 'Lord's Supper', we make our own Jesus's will to unite all humanity round the Father's Table, building up the Mystical Body which will be completed after the last Mass on earth, when the veil of faith will be torn aside and the Redeemed admitted to the eternal Banquet of Heaven.

Chapter Twenty

THE REVELATION OF GOD

The path of prayer is as long as man's life, neither more nor less. It is now a glorious path through the meadows, now a peaceful country road with no obstacles where we can abandon ourselves to quiet thought, now a rough mule-track winding up the mountains, now a way over the bare rocks on the summit. Sometimes it is like a city street full of noise and distraction, at others it follows the water off the streets into underground drains and so to the river or sea, carrying with it the rubbish and filth of life.

But it is always prayer.

It is still prayer, I believe, even when it is silence and looks to the observer like the dried-up bed of a stream. Surely a blade of grass bent with the heat is still a prayer in Heaven's eyes even though it cannot ask for water?

Surely the pitiable state of someone reduced to running sores by loneliness and evil is a prayer, even though he says nothing but speaks with his life?

It is difficult for a God who is Love not to find a pretext for intervention and assistance in the affairs of His poor creature – man – who prior to sin made the mistake of being in too great a hurry to reach his final end, God, and after sin made the further mistake of no longer being able to believe in such a glorious end for himself.

God, however, hears man's prayer, He hears it whatever its nature.

He hears it when it is expressed in words, He helps it when it becomes thought and meditation, He supports and animates it when it finally becomes life.

That is not enough, however.

Man's destiny goes far beyond this world, beyond the limits of human life. Speech and thought belong to an earth-bound way of life, they are activities which cannot reach beyond death, cannot attain the Transcendence of God.

If our destiny is to meet God and contemplate Him face to face beyond worldly symbols, in His naked reality, we need a prayer more appropriate to God's level, of the same nature as God, in other words, a supernatural form of prayer. We have been given this in infused contemplation.

During man's pilgrimage of faith, God first reveals Himself in symbol, and man can therefore talk to Him as he does to his fellows and think of Him in largely human ways. But even at the very limit of this revelation, man knows that he has seen not God but – how shall I put it? – His garment.

Everything we know about God is not God but a pointer, an image.

And it is here that man discovers his total poverty, the abyss which separates him from his transcendent Lord, his absolute inability to reach and possess God.

In this time of waiting, the only new dimension that can be added to prayer is silence, which transcends all other dimensions and which, to enable man to receive and welcome God in His Word (which is no longer created but, in Christ, uncreated), becomes a painful, dry, crucified silence. God's real self-revelation to man takes place in this framework of man's absolute poverty and powerlessness, the image of which is the aridity of the desert.

We can do nothing beyond that to make progress. Our words turn to lamentation, and even meditation, which was so deep and lively at the beginning, will fall silent in its absolute impotence. At that moment God's true revelation to man begins. Having realized to the point of pain his absolute poverty and dryness, man opens himself to God like a flower in the humidity of night.

Then God reveals Himself to man, 'lifts the veil', makes Himself known, not in human terms, with human images and symbols, but in wordless terms, with images and symbols that go beyond every symbol. It is revelation at God's level, what we call supernatural revelation. Contemplation is in fact defined as the 'rapid, dark and supernatural revelation of God'.

Infused contemplation, which begins here on earth at the exact moment of the soul's maturity in the heat of the divine sun, will continue in eternity and constitute the plenitude of our union with God. If I am asked whether eternal life is just love of God, I reply without hesitation, *'it is, above all, knowledge'*.

There can be no love without knowledge; love is the fruit of knowledge.

Everything therefore begins with knowledge. To make us love Him God must first make us know Him, and if we did not have this real, supernatural if obscure knowledge of God, we could never love and so possess Him.

This is why He reveals Himself to His friends.

Did He never tell us all this?

Of course He did.

At the Last Supper, when He was about to leave His own, Jesus exclaimed:

> 'Anybody who receives my commandments and
> keeps them will be one who loves me;
> and anybody who loves me will be loved by my
>   Father,
> and I shall love him and show myself to him.'

(Jn 14:21)

How can you say you will 'show yourself' to us when you are leaving us, leaving us for ever?

128

And yet it will be so, because the promised revelation will not require Jesus's physical presence. It will be a new thing not fashioned with words of this world. It will be part of *'a mysterious, personal communication without images, without any mediation between God and the soul'*: it will be the Holy Spirit's revelation to man.

It will be a revelation of eternal, supernatural light, disclosing to man the Father's face, the Son's face, the Spirit's face.

It will be the anticipation of Paradise, a proof of the existence of the transcendent God and man's ability to communicate with Him now that he has become a sharer in the divine life, which is eternal life.

Moses had an 'experience' of it in front of the burning bush when God revealed His name: 'I Am who I Am' (Ex 3:14).

Elijah 'felt' it when, after his trial in the wilderness, God revealed Himself on Horeb in the sound of a gentle breeze (1 K 19:12).

The psalmist informs us of God's presence when he exclaims:

> My soul thirsts for God,
>   the God of life;
> when shall I go to see
>   the face of God?

> (Ps 42:2)

and again:

> Yes, with you is the fountain of life,
> by your light we see the light.

> (Ps 36:9)

and again, when he is seized by this living Presence and sees his soul's destiny:

> Yahweh, my heart has no lofty ambitions,
>   my eyes do not look too high.

I am not concerned with great affairs
    or marvels beyond my scope.
Enough for me to keep my soul tranquil and quiet
    like a child in its mother's arms,
as content as a child that has been weaned.

        (Ps 131:1–2)

The person whose contemplation is his life does not need many words to pray.

He needs one word, at the most two . . . I am not trying to make some sort of joke: his one word of prayer will be enough to sum up everything he wishes to say once his whole life, in its deepest intimacy,. has been transformed into prayer.

Let me explain.

Because man's prayer on earth is a tension between God's greatness and man's smallness, between the abyss of the Absolute and the abyss of our nothingness, between the incommunicability of the divine Transcendence and the possessed irrationality of sin, man feels the need to cast his prayer up like a flaming arrow towards the divine Mystery or down into the abyss of sin, the expression of his deepest wretchedness.

He therefore feels urged both to cry his thirst for the Almighty with a word which is the name of God and to remind himself of the state of his soul which is 'sin'.

He needs only these two words which he forges into steel darts that seek to pierce the Cloud of God's Unknowing, thereby expressing all the insatiability of his prayer.

God,

Sin, the English mystics used to say.

Kyrie eleison, pomiliu Gospodi, say the Greeks and Russians in the long litanies so typical of their liturgy.

The Latins more often express this drama of love in other ways:

Jesus, I love You,
have mercy on me.

And it is certainly magnificent to remain there, one's whole soul poised between those two phrases, with no other wish than to throw oneself towards the Cloud of Unknowing and pierce it with the sheer force of one's love; than to throw oneself towards the Cloud which conceals God in His naked Being and which the soul seeks in the darkness of faith without considering itself and without distractions from external things.

Nothing can be more profitable than this loving effort on the soul's part sharpened to one word of prayer.

Nothing is more useful for the person concerned and his loved ones, for the living and dead, for the whole Church.

Nothing is more definitive for people during their earthly pilgrimage, nothing better sums up their 'contemplation on the road'.

The person who has reached this position needs only continue without deviating to right or left. He knows that 'what is to come must come thence'.

When St Thomas, at the completion of his work on the *Summa*, had a momentary experience in prayer of God's Transcendence concealed in the Cloud of Unknowing, he cried out in ecstasy: 'Everything I have written is but straw.'

Not that straw is useless, and well he knew it!

Without it, without the long stem, how can the ear on top reach up to open itself to the action of God's sun?

Theology, culture, philosophy, science are the human stem slowly bearing the ear of our soul towards the warmth of the divine sun.

But once the ear lies in the sun and begins to open with the approach of autumn, the stem becomes straw because its work is finished and the soul needs nothing but sun before being harvested into God's eternal granary.

Chapter Twenty-One

GOD'S LOVE IN US

When someone on earth has reached the state of contemplation, lives contemplation, he is finally at peace, like a child on its mother's breast: 'My soul is tranquil and quiet like a child in its mother's arms' (Ps 131:2).

Magnetized by God's love, the rocket of his soul, like an astronaut's space-craft, has broken the sound-barrier (no longer needs a lot of words to explain itself), snapped the thread of gravity which held it down to itself (no longer needs meditation) and gone into orbit like a tiny planet round God's sun.

He can say with the psalmist: 'I am as content as a child that has been weaned' (Ps 131:2).

The first proof that someone has gone into orbit round God is that he no longer feels he himself is the *centre of the universe* – which is the real nature of sin – but feels and vividly understands that God is the centre of everything. This might seem easy, but . . . how much effort goes into reaching this understanding!

Now at last God bears him, leads him by 'ways which are not our ways', draws him into the whirlpool of charity, prepares him for an ever deeper union with Himself, for that eternal possession of Himself which is the goal of our human-divine destiny.

The soul in orbit round God begins to realize that there is another stability than the kind known and experienced on earth, another fulness, another dimension. Above all, another 'peace'.

The peace promised by Jesus:

> 'my own peace I give you,
> a peace the world cannot give.'

(Jn 14:27)

And this peace communicates to the soul such a sense of 'new life', such a 'chaste joy' despite the tremendous trials of the spatial flight round God, such a richness of hope in 'what is to come' despite the crosses of every day, that the soul can exclaim with St Francis:

> So great is the good that even pain is a delight.

That is quite something!

At bottom, what is the real difficulty in living on earth?

Is it not surmounting pain, fear, illness, old age, death? Well, if we have found something which enables us to overcome these negative aspects of our earthly pilgrimage, which helps us to smile through our tears, to hope even as we slowly decline, to be certain of life even in death, we have experienced in ourselves the victory brought by Christ.

> 'I have conquered the world.'

(Jn 16:33)

Christ's victory is love bestowed on us in its divine dimension which is called 'charity'. If we are in charity God is in us, and charity is the fruit of contemplation as love is the fruit of knowledge.

Revealing Himself to us in contemplation, God communicates charity, that is, His love, and by living this love of His we live in Him and share in His 'victory' during our struggle on earth, just as we shall share in the beatific possession of Him 'above', when every struggle will be at an end.

133

It is said that 'love conquers everything' – *omnia vincit amor*.
And it is true.

Yes, love conquers everything, always.

It conquers even the most horrible things.

Like Jesus's life.

Is it not horrible to be born in a stable a few hours after the
citizens of Bethlehem had refused to give lodging to His
mother who was near her time and was looking for a minimum
of warmth because otherwise she ran the risk of seeing her
child die with cold in the night?

Well, Mary's and Joseph's love and willingness to put up
with these horrible things gave the world the 'Christmas Story'
which has made the hardest hearts dissolve in tears and which
is the irreplaceable masterpiece and the authentic account of
God's infinity and omnipotence enclosed in the tiny body of a
baby at the mercy of history.

Is it not horrible, men's treatment of Jesus during His life
and in His death? Is Calvary not horrible?

Well, Jesus's love transformed the horror of it into sublimity. His acceptance, His humility, His meekness changed
the aspect of things, and the most obscene chapter in history
becomes the most beautiful, the most tender, the most
grandiose, the most exemplary, the most alluring, in which a
dying God smiles on man who is killing Him and pardons him.

Only love, of all things in heaven and on earth, has such
transforming, sublimating, redeeming, enriching, life-giving
power!

Love is superior to everything else, can substitute for
everything else, by touching what man on earth cannot attain:
perfection. As St Paul says: 'Charity is the bond which makes us
perfect' (Col 3:14, Knox).

Having convinced myself of the primacy of charity, having
become aware that in touching charity I am touching God,
that in living charity I am living God in me, I must this
evening, before finishing my meditation, look at tomorrow to

subject it to this light and live it out under the inspiration of this synthesis of love. Basically I must do what Jesus – who brought God's love to earth and communicated it to us – would do in my position. I must remember that the opportunities I shall have to suffer, to pardon, to accept are treasures not to be lost through distraction and values that I must make my own as a worthy response to God's plan in creation.

My life is worth living if I can learn to transform everything that happens to me into love, in imitation of Jesus: because *love is for living*.

When I meet a brother of mine who has caused me great pain in the past by viciously calumniating me, I shall love him, and in loving him I shall transform the evil done to me into good: because *love is for living*.

When I have to live with people who do not see things the way I see them, who say they are enemies of my faith, I shall love them, and in loving them I shall sow the seeds of future dialogue in my heart and theirs: because *love is for living*.

When I go into a shop to buy something for myself – clothes, food, or whatever it may be – I shall think of my brothers who are poorer than I am, of the hungry and the naked, and I shall use this thought to govern my purchases, trying out of love to be tight with myself and generous with them: because *love is for living*.

When I see time's destructive traces in my body and the approach of old age, I shall try to love even more in order to transform the coldest season of life into a total gift of myself in preparation for the imminent holocaust: because *love is for living*.

When I see the evening of my life, or, on the tarmac in a car accident, in the agony of a fatal illness, in the ward of a geriatric hospital, feel the end coming, I shall reach out again for love, striving to accept in joy whatever fate God has had in store for me: because *love is for living*.

Yes, love is God in me, and if I am in love I am in God, that is, in life, in grace: a sharer in God's being.

No one has seen this so clearly and expressed it so forcibly as St Paul:

If I have all the eloquence of men or of angels, but speak without love, I am simply a gong booming or a cymbal clashing. If I have the gift of prophecy, understanding all the mysteries there are, and knowing everything, and if I have faith in all its fulness, to move mountains, but without love, then I am nothing at all. If I give away all that I possess, piece by piece, and if I even let them take my body to burn it, but am without love, it will do me no good whatever.

Love is always patient and kind; it is never jealous; love is never boastful or conceited; it is never rude or selfish; it does not take offence, and is not resentful. Love takes no pleasure in other people's sins but delights in the truth; it is always ready to excuse, to trust, to hope, and to endure whatever comes.

(1 Co 13:1–7)

Could any words be clearer?

If charity is God in me, why look for God any further than myself?

And if He is in me as love, why do I change or disfigure His face with acts or values which are not love?

PART IV

We are now approaching the end of our road.

We have meditated on the various degrees of human love and the mysterious way in which charity, which is the divine dimension of love, takes hold of us.

We are left with three meditations which, though very simple, are vitally important because they concern Jesus's deepest desire, which He Himself defined as '*His commandment*'.

Chapter Twenty-Two

THE NEW COMMANDMENT

The ancients were right when they said that there was nothing new under the sun, because they had as yet no knowledge of the only new thing that could happen, the only Person capable of producing something new: Jesus.

Jesus contradicted the old adage because He was something new under the sun, the only new thing there could be.

There was even something new in love!

In olden times it was said: 'You shall love your neighbour as yourself', and that was perfectly logical. Love being the proper response to a value and men being of equal value, it was right to love others as oneself, even at great cost to oneself.

Theoretically it is obvious. Your skin is as important as mine, I must love the two equally; your hunger is as important as mine, I must satisfy it with the same bread; your nakedness is as regrettable as mine, I must prevent it with the same degree of concern. And so on.

To get this far is no mean feat, and the difficulty in putting it into practice betrays the imbalance and disorder of sin in us; it is the proof that we are ill, that our priorities are fundamentally wrong, because otherwise the equation 'love for you = love for myself' would be almost automatically put into practice.

The person who loves himself and not others, who feeds himself and not others, who clothes himself and not others is a 'mistake', an 'aberration', and he must correct himself if he wishes to enter the Kingdom, which is a Kingdom of Truth. It is impossible to gain entrance to the Kingdom of God, which means equality, with inequality in one's mind, heart or will.

We have a lifetime in which to correct the error – with the help of grace – and if we have not managed it here we shall continue to try hereafter. One way or another, the books must be in order before the Master arrives to inspect them.

And this particular Master is not easily satisfied in matters of love!

He seems to be in such a hurry!

Jesus reveals to the people of the old Law, the fulfilment of which was already very difficult because of sin, another type of love which He jealously defines as 'His commandment'. This new commandment is not human but divine, and it expresses in all its splendour the height of perfection to which Jesus wishes to lead us:

'You also must love one another just as I have loved you.'

(Jn 13:34)

It was already difficult to establish equality; Jesus went further.

'Love as I have loved, that is, to the ultimate sacrifice, to the total gift of yourself.'

The past had spent all its time establishing justice in human relationships: one for me and one for you, a slap in the face for me and a slap in the face for you, an eye for an eye and a tooth for a tooth. Jesus comes on the scene and shouts: 'But *I* tell you!'

What does He tell us?

'Love your enemies, do good to those who hate you, bless those who curse you, pray for those who treat you badly. To the man who slaps you on the cheek, present the other cheek too; to the man who takes your cloak from you, do not refuse your tunic. Give to everyone who asks you, and do not ask for your property back from the man who robs you.'

(Lk 6:27–30)

No, humanity did not have to wait for Gandhi to discover non-violence! But perhaps the human race – mitred gorillas, as Merton called them – was not ready for it.

Today Jesus would have been condemned as a proponent of man's right to conscientious objection.

It is always too early for a prophet to say certain things; always too late at death to put Jesus's teaching into practice if, out of laziness or cowardice, we have not done so already.

The Gospel should be prohibited: it should be a banned book in civilized countries, especially those of established bourgeois culture. It is an uncomfortable book for pagans and an even more uncomfortable one for Christians. It denounces us continually, its tremendous words pronounce judgement on the centuries. Theologians will expatiate on the justice of war, saints will preach crusades, Christians will bear arms as readily as they bear the cross and will fight as if it were cardboard puppets they were running through.

Mystery of contradiction! Undisputed sign of our littleness! Evident testimony of the infinite superiority of the Gospel over poor human history! Astronomical distance between the word of God and man's morality! But . . . wait a moment: I have the impression there is something new under the sun . . .

Giovanni Papini made a sort of prophecy in his old age. He suggested that each year of Jesus's life corresponded to a century of Church history. This would mean that we have entered our twenty-first year, the year of our majority.

Perhaps we have; the Second Vatican Council is a sign of it.

And perhaps a few Christians are beginning to accept proper responsibility and take Jesus's words seriously:

'To the man who slaps you on one cheek, present the other cheek too; to the man who takes your cloak from you, do not refuse your tunic.'

(Lk 6:29)

Now that is not child's play! Who is really capable of taking

Jesus's words seriously? Who really believes this kind of teaching? It is too easy to think: 'Well, what He really meant by this was . . .' or 'taken metaphorically this would mean . . .' And because we cannot take Jesus literally, we have managed in the space of thirty years two world wars that have bled Europe with weapons blessed by the various religions!

Perhaps we needed the discovery of atomic energy and the apocalypse that would ensue if nuclear war broke out before we began to wonder whether, after all . . . *even a war of defence would be unjustifiable because of the frightful consequences even of defence.*

In other words, Jesus was right.

But Jesus's teaching applies equally in such relatively minor incidents as a blow in the face and a stolen cloak! Is the peace which results from yielding to violence on the part of a brother not worth more than the cloak?

Do the advantages that accrue from pardoning his use of violence and doing without law-courts and lawyers not outweigh the value of the tunic? I know that it is difficult to talk like this because we suffer from a surfeit not of 'love' but of 'justice', while Jesus suffers from love and wishes to win the battle of justice with love.

We are trying to reconcile two different positions, and this is probably why, after centuries of disquisitions on morality, we have forged a moral theology which leaves us bewildered and in which few people still really believe.

It is probably why there is a shindy whenever conscientious objection makes the news. The sad thing is that young men who refuse to bear arms are imprisoned. I confess that I fail to follow the reasoning here, and in this specific case I should merely repeat the Council's wise words:

It seems right that laws make humane provisions for the case of those who for reasons of conscience refuse to bear arms. (*Gaudium et Spes* 79)

We should lose nothing by forming young conscientious objectors into 'peace corps' to reconstruct villages destroyed in earthquakes, give schooling to illiterate people, bring assistance to lepers or the starving. In peace-time there is no problem. But in war? It is better to say nothing here for fear of infuriating the 'moderates', the defenders of established order, nationalist fanatics. But one tiny plea I shall make. Members of government, think twice before declaring war. That is all I ask: think twice!

It could be that *not* declaring war is the better solution. Take extreme care.

You might entrust an atomic bomb to a pilot who drops it in the middle of the sea without a detonator; or you might give bayonets to youngsters who use them to cut flowers to welcome the arriving enemy: 'please come in, won't you? there's coffee ready.'

You will no doubt call me a defeatist.

I suppose it is a question of deciding whether the young Austrian who preferred to be condemned to death by a military tribunal rather than take up arms with Hitler was a martyr or a traitor.

It is a question of deciding whether the few voices raised against Mussolini in protest at his invasion of Ethiopia were more Christian than the screams of the masses intoxicated by an undiscriminating nationalism and blinded by colossal historical ignorance.

It is a question of deciding whether those who in Algeria refused to obey orders to torture prisoners in the service of victory at any price were defeatists or Christians.

In short, it is a question of deciding whether someone has the right to trample on my conscience merely because he is in charge, whether the State can force me to take part in its schemes ... when they are evil.

Perhaps as never before the moment has come in which we shall see blossoming in a soil ploughed by the atrocious suffering of thousands of wars the flower of man's conscience able to stand firm not only in defence of belief in Christ, as in times past, but – and this would be new – in defence of belief in man.

I am wasting time, however, talking about things that will never happen: there will not be any real wars again.

I must talk instead to those who believe in Jesus, who look for the happiness of peace – 'happy the peacemakers: they shall be called sons of God' (Mt 5:9) – who have no need to puff their chests out and strike their neighbour in the face, who know they are small and weak, in short, to the poor, and I have something very important to say.

Do you want to know the secret of true happiness? of deep and genuine peace?

Do you want to solve at a blow all your difficulties in relations with your neighbour, bring all polemic to an end, avoid all dissension?

Well, decide here and now to love things and men as Jesus loved them, that is, to the point of self-sacrifice.

Don't bother with the book-keeping of love; love without keeping accounts.

If you know someone who is decent and likeable, love him, but if someone else is very *un*likeable, love him just the same.

If someone greets you and smiles, greet him and smile back, but if someone else treads on your feet, smile just the same. If someone does you a good turn, thank the Lord for it, but if someone else slanders you, persecutes you, curses you, strikes you, thank him and carry on.

Do not say: 'I'm right, he's wrong.' Say: 'I must love him as myself.' This is the kind of love Jesus taught: a love which transforms, vivifies, enriches, brings peace.

Love is not an easy thing, and I should like to say to those who decide to tread this path of love: 'take courage and stand firm; be well prepared and go with the help of grace, because the journey is long and you will have shed blood before the end of it. You'll be lucky to get there the minute before you die.'

144

Every day I beg the Lord to grant me one grace in particular: to love and learn to love as He has done!

To love as Jesus did at Bethlehem when He fled into exile rather than use His divine omnipotence to kill Herod.

To love as Jesus did at Nazareth, where He lived as the last of men without appealing to His incarnate and hidden divinity.

To love as Jesus did at the sight of the hungry, shepherdless crowd, with a greater determination to solve the problem with sacrifice than with miracles and glory.

To love as Jesus did in Gethsemane when for our sake He endured the frightful agony of His loneliness and the Father's condemnation.

To love as Jesus did before the Sanhedrin when, with His silence and His acceptance of condemnation and rejection, He gave us the exact measure of His power of love.

To love as Jesus did on Calvary, when, at the height of His passion and already in the last throes of death, He prayed His last prayer to Heaven: 'Father, forgive them.'

This is the supreme life, and Jesus lived it in all His splendour and superhuman power.

He loved without setting a limit.

And He invites us to do the same; nothing else matters so much as this.

Why do we wrap ourselves up in a juridical and narrow Christianity, occupy our minds with an exasperating casuistry which no longer convinces anyone, instead of throwing ourselves down towards men with only love in our hearts?

Why, after Jesus's mission on earth, do we insist on the defence of justice when justice alone is not able to save us?

We have the *right* but not the *duty* to defend ourselves, and we can very well waive it as an offering to love, pardon, peace, dialogue with men.

No?

Oh, how I wish the Church born from the Council will be a

Church concerned less with the length of girls' skirts and more with the problems posed by love in the world; a Church capable of giving more than of receiving, a Church which, for love of men, can renounce its own rights and privileges, a Church which dispenses with self-defence and travels the road of its exile as small and poor as Jesus's family on their flight to Egypt.

Chapter Twenty-Three

THE FIRE OF PURGATORY

If the Master should knock on my door tonight and tell me that my earthly pilgrimage is at an end, I feel that on balance I should not be consigned to hell.

Why?

Because neither God nor myself wishes it, He for love of me, I for love of Him. Despite immense evil in me, I feel, in the strength of His love, the desire to be with Him, and this seems to me to be quite normal between friends. I know sin as ignorance and even more so as weakness, but I have never felt 'opposed' to God. I cannot even visualize – thanks to His grace – the 'sin against the Holy Spirit'; I cannot imagine how someone could impugn the known truth. Theologians discuss it at length, but their subtleties do not impress me.

I was saying, then, that if I died today, I should not on balance be condemned to an eternity of torment. But then neither should I be admitted to Heaven! I am not ready for it. I felt that very, very keenly under the rock when I had denied Kadà my blanket, and I still feel it today, Good Friday, as I meditate on our Lord's passion. Yes, I am afraid to suffer for others, I tremble before the cold blade of charity.

And so? If I am not to go to hell and Heaven is too good for me, where shall I go?

I must stay here, I cannot pass beyond, and purgatory is certainly this side of the eternal watershed.

I am not a theologian, but even theologians know little about purgatory. It is a passing place or state or condition in which those not yet ready for the Kingdom of Perfect Love pray and suffer and so prepare themselves for the day when they will be admitted to the eternal banquet.

I imagine purgatory to be like the large cupboard where my grandmother put medlars to ripen. Please forgive this curious comparison. When I was young, I occasionally stayed at my grandmother's house, which was a farm in the Langhe hills of Piedmont, and I remember my grandmother putting the medlars which were still not ripe by the autumn into this cupboard, amongst the straw. 'Everything comes to him who waits.' A spiritual fruit that has failed to ripen under the sun of God's charity will ripen in the cupboard.

The comparison is perhaps a good one because the cupboard is part of the house.

I should not like to offend anyone's sensibilities, and so I say this from a purely personal point of view, but I think of purgatory as being this side of eternity and therefore still tied to my home. I think of the souls of the dead completing their period of expiation near where they lived, perhaps even in their homes themselves. If I can make a request at the moment of death, I know what I shall ask: 'Send me to the stretch of desert between Tit and Silet', where I had the deepest insight into the need for perfect love at the earliest possible moment.

And the fire? Ah, I thought that question would come.

Well, I think there is fire but not of a material kind. Many times as a boy, especially in the sacristies of mountain churches, I have seen the souls in purgatory wrapped in flames – real flames – with fiery tongues higher than the highest heads there. It is natural for artists to think and paint in this way: how else could one depict the spiritual fire of purgatory? In the Middle Ages, and since, the flames are always shown as real ones, simply because it is easier that way.

Everyone, however, knows that real fire would damage the body ... and the body is not in purgatory but in the cemetery, like a piece of cast-off clothing.

To touch my soul another type of fire is necessary: charity, which I rejected on earth, or at least did not fully accept. Now that I have my back to the wall, I cannot escape it any longer, I must accept it. I cannot put it off any more.

The fire of charity, that is, this supernatural kind of love, will attack my soul as flames attack wood. My soul will writhe, sizzle and smoke like green wood, but it will burn in the end. Not a single fibre shall escape, all must be consumed by that divine love.

How long will this take? It will go on until the work is done. Some people will need no more than a few days, others thousands of years; the important thing is that the purification must be completed. All this will take place while a sort of film of our lives is screened before our eyes.

There is more than enough there. When I think that I shall have to relive in slow motion certain episodes in my life which I did not subject to the flames of love but constructed on egoism, falsehood, cowardice and pride, and all the time with the fire of charity in my veins, I can assure you that it comes home to me what a serious, deadly serious, business it will be. Imagine me arriving in purgatory wearing a mask put together with years of patience and skill which I have never dared or been able to remove for fear of revealing myself as I really am to God and men.

When the fire of love licks up at it, gets beneath it and burns it off my soul, it will, I have no doubt, prove an agonizing experience. And what will happen when the fire starts to burn the property to which I was clinging so firmly: a blanket perhaps, or a piece of meat I took first from the plate when Jesus would have wanted me to be last?

No, there is no need for a coal fire to burn my soul: the fire of failed responsibility, of injustices, of thefts, of lies, of help denied to someone who needed me, of love not lived with those who were my brothers, is more than sufficient.

Not very much, you say? Well, that is only a part of it, the part we can imagine by the standards of earthly justice. True justice, measured on God's justice, on the Transcendence of the Absolute, appalled St John of the Cross when he was undergoing the terrors of the dark night of the soul.

Yes, the fire of purgatory is charity, that is, the highest degree of love in its supernatural state.

It is the fire which consumed Jesus's sacrifice on Calvary, the fire which burned the saints with inextinguishable love, the fire which led the martyrs to martyrdom and baptized them if they were not already baptized, giving them access to the Kingdom. We shall not escape this fire, nothing we do can avert it.

On the other hand I should not wish to escape it. I know it will hurt, but I also know that I have to go through it.

I have no desire to continue for all eternity the ups and downs of my sensibility, the perennial resistance to the fire of love. I am green wood, and I do not wish to enter Paradise still green. I want to burn in purgatory and then be finished with it.

I want to go where Jesus went, to feel what He felt in His divine heart. I shall suffer, I know, but there is no other way, and in any case God's power will be there beside me to bring me assistance.

Here and now I accept that fire which will smelt from me and my earthly slag the hidden metal of my person, willed by God but obscured by sin.

I shall be given a new face, the face that God saw when He drew me from the primeval chaos and that Satan sullied with his slaver.

I shall emerge a child, God's child for ever.

And since purgatory is this side of the eternal watershed, the only appropriate course for me is to combine it with my life on earth, pretend I am already there, apply the fire of charity to myself a little at a time but courageously, start to burn out the clinkers, at least the biggest and most obvious ones.

What I do here I shall not need to do hereafter: I have

therefore gained. I must accept the asceticism my life imposes on me, the sufferings and trials I experience on the road, the tedium and troubles of human society, the inconveniences and inevitable illnesses as precious and providential opportunities for advance payment.

I say 'opportunities', because there is more to paying than suffering. One must suffer with love, with patience, otherwise it is useless. We were saved not by the scourges on Jesus's flesh but by the love with which He accepted them.

We were redeemed not by His road to Calvary but by the patience, mercy, obedience with which He trod it.

In short, the Redemption renewed the world by Jesus's charity. Charity is the essence of Christianity. Yes, we can state with absolute certainty that *love is for living*.

And if we can transform every moment of our existence into an act of love, all our problems will be resolved. The fire of purgatory is love, and if we wish to avoid purgatory, we must accept its fire on earth.

Chapter Twenty-Four

COME, LORD!

The only course open to us now is to wait.

Whatever can or will happen belongs not to us but to Christ.

And we have one great hope, which should sustain us beyond all our poor human efforts. On Calvary Jesus uttered this astounding phrase in reply to the Good Thief: 'Indeed I promise you, today you will be with me in paradise' (Lk 23:43).

Today . . . today . . . today . . . today!

This word echoes in my soul's ear like a message of hope, a shout of joy.

Today!

What about all our own calculations?

And I talked about thousands of years to be spent in purgatory!

It is possible – indeed certain – that the Good Thief was more prepared than I am to enter the Kingdom of Perfect Love, because of my incurable egoism, but . . .

No, weighing the pros and cons is an earthly not a heavenly activity, it belongs to justice not to the gratuity of love.

No, eternity is not the sum of all possible centuries, infinity is not a succession of spatial units, and grace is not the fruit or reward of a sufficient amount of effort on man's part. Eternity is eternity, infinity infinity, and grace grace, that is, gratuitous, absolutely gratuitous.

It is a mystery, and we must accept it in its totality if we do not wish to lose our way in the darkness of the human mind.

There have been saints who felt the fire of hell at their feet all their lives and could talk of nothing else; others preferred not to emphasize it because they could think of nothing but the resplendent fire of the divine mercy.

In His divine teaching Jesus Himself seems to have taken care not to be too precise, limiting Himself to stressing the essential, what we need to know and should not forget.

There is nothing to be done, therefore. We must not ask too many questions on the how and how much of purgatory, otherwise we shall oblige the Divine Master to answer us as He answered the over-curious apostles: 'As for that day and hour, nobody knows it, neither the angels in heaven, nor the Son, no one but the Father only' (Mt 24:36).

What we *do* know from Jesus's clear teaching is this: 'Stay awake and stand ready' (Mt 24:42, 44); 'be like men waiting for their master to return from the wedding feast, ready to open the door as soon as he comes and knocks' (Lk 12:36).

In the Gospel and in the thought of St John and St Paul who were Jesus's most passionate and accurate interpreters in the first Christian communities, there was a typical feature: the profound and dramatic sense of 'expectation', the expectation of an extraordinary event which would renew the face of the earth: 'Now I am making the whole of creation new' (Rv 21:5), and a surprise even for the most vigilant: 'I shall come to you like a thief' (Rv 3:3), like 'lightning flashing from one part of heaven to the other' (Lk 17:24).

Apart from the exaggeration of a number of early Christians who interpreted 'the expectation' as Christ's imminent return, a 'parousia' soon to take place, because of the impatience of their love, such a deeply evangelical attitude seems to me to be the most appropriate and the truest for all who wish to enter into the spirit of the things of God and live on this earth as a preparation for the eternal season of heaven.

The Christian life is an expectation, a waiting for something, a continual movement from one point to another.

When we pray, we are waiting for something. When we act, we are waiting for something.

What is perfect if not a tireless and endless motion from the limited to the Infinite, from man to God?

It is expectation.

And expectation is primarily an awareness that things do not depend on us.

This is vital because it gives us access to true humility, to truth. Things do not depend on us, the result does not depend on us, salvation does not depend on us.

'When I open, nobody can close, and when I close, nobody can open', says Christ in the Apocalypse (Rv 3:7).

It was the most dramatic element in the conversion of St Paul, who was deeply Hebrew and a profound believer in the Law.

Salvation comes not from the law and efforts to observe it but from God's gratuitous love.

We are justified not by our works but by faith and the promise.

This affects the balance of the entire God-man relationship, and we have to be very small and helpless in the Father's arms if we do not wish to suffer from giddiness.

Salvation, then, is not my doing.

Just as something dramatic had to happen if the Israelites were to cross the Reed Sea dryshod, so some new event which does not depend on me must take place in my soul as I strain towards love. I shall not be the one to stand on my grave and shout, 'Rise up': Christ will, no one else.

This, I think, brings me to the end of this book, and in order to conclude these meditations with a modicum of order I should like to invoke the help of our Lady, who of all creatures saw things clearly because of all creatures she was the smallest and the humblest.

You will remember that it all began one day in a small piece of desert in the solitude of the Sahara, when I dreamt I was being crushed by a great mass of granite under which I had gone to sleep.

I stood condemned at God's judgement-seat, and I was condemned for lack of love: nothing else.

A blanket withheld from a poor man sent me on my way to purgatory, and there I realized that to leave purgatory I should have to perform some act of perfect love, that is, an act of the same kind as Jesus's love.

I felt it was beyond me.

Many years have passed since then, and yesterday, Good Friday, meditating on Jesus's passion, I found myself in the same position as that time beneath the rock.

I cannot love perfectly, I have not the strength to follow Jesus to Calvary.

Should I ever feel I could?

If I thought I had the strength to, should I not be even worse than I am?

That is the truth I have finally discovered in my long and hard religious experience.

If my salvation depended on me, I should never be saved!

Something must happen first: a flash of lightning, a visit from someone, an event.

And I shall never be able to discover it, anticipate it, foresee it!

I must wait, praying, loving, weeping, beseeching.

This is all man can do on earth and in purgatory.

God, who is God of the impossible, will come unexpectedly and touching my soul will make me capable of following Him wherever He has decided to lead me like the Good Thief on that first Good Friday.

And by the time I discover I am capable, I shall already be beyond death and I shall have no time to admire myself like Narcissus and therefore destroy in pride the gratuity of the grace which has produced in me the power to love as Jesus loved.

In *The Dialogue of the Carmelites*, Bernanos depicts two very different nuns. One represents tenacity, strength, will-power; the other smallness and weakness.

In death it is the latter who wins through, managing to sing as she mounts the guillotine.

The other will always be afraid of death – even in her bed.

On the other hand, if we accept the thesis of victorious weakness, of the thief who gains Paradise at the last moment, of the person whose whole life is prayer and in some sense inactivity, do we not run the risk of quietism, of the lack of human commitment, of idleness and inaction?

If we accept the thesis that it is faith which justifies and not our effort and apostolate, are we not raking up the age-old dispute that has so painfully divided Christians?

No, not at all, if we give this approach its proper value, which the Church in its divine balance has always done, supported as it is by the Spirit of God.

Jesus's words are always normative in the search for truth:

'See that you are dressed for action and have your lamps lit. Be like men waiting for their master to return from the wedding feast, ready to open the door as soon as he comes and knocks. Happy those servants whom the master finds awake when he comes.'

(Lk 12:35–7a)

Attentive, dynamic, virile and passionate vigilance is all here.

To be quite ready the servant does not even sit down for fear of dozing off.

Matthew records the same words:

'What sort of servant, then, is faithful and wise enough for the master to place him over his household to give them their food at the proper time? Happy that servant if his master's arrival finds him at this employment.'

(Mt 24:45–6)

That is the real significance of waiting: 'the master will find him at this employment'.

Criticism of the mystical life, of prayer, of contemplation is shown to be totally unfounded where Matthew 24:46 is verified:

'the master will find him at this employment.'

Teilhard de Chardin says that God's will is on the point of my effort, on the point of my pencil, on the point of my plough – powerful imagery to express the fact that man must act, that the Christian must exert himself to the full.

God gives Himself to the person who acts and acts as if he were immobile. God communicates Himself to the person who looks for Him knowing that the search would be in vain if God were not looking for him at the same time. St Ignatius, who was a great contemplative, summed up the problem as follows:

'Act as if everything depended on you and wait as if everything depended on God.'

And Don Bosco, who combined authentic mysticism and action to a remarkable degree, displayed his supernatural equilibrium when, tired of running about after ministers, he went to sleep in their antechambers. This response to the difficulties of conversation with the important ones of the world seems to me to be the clearest sign of Don Bosco's contemplative soul totally surrendered to the Father. And it also seems to me to be the clearest indication for us Christians today that having to live in the spirit of the Council which God's infinite Providence bestowed on His ever youthful, fresh and fertile Church we run the risk – as Paul VI put it so aptly – of losing our sense of balance in the interplay of opposing forces.

Action or thought?
Prayer or evangelization?
Speech or witness?
I think we have already given the answer.

May the strong wind of the Spirit, which blew so vigorously through the Church at the Council, bring us the divine power, and may God guide us with sweetness and strength on the roads of the modern world.

OTHER ORBIS TITLES BY THE SAME AUTHOR

LETTERS FROM THE DESERT

"Carretto's most beautiful and most powerful expressions of faith are found in his reflections on love and man's soul." *Concern.*

"This book is a gem—from the sands of the Sahara!"
Homiletic & Pastoral Review

ISBN 0-88344-2795 Cloth $4.95

THE GOD WHO COMES

"Carlo Carretto was a young Italian activist who discovered the writings of Father Charles de Foucauld. He gave up everything and went to the Sahara to join the Little Brothers, hermits who followed de Foucauld's spiritual way. In this, his second book, he shares the magnificant Catholic reflections that have inspired him. He sees strength for the Church in these times of change. As most contemplatives do, he has discovered that by withdrawing from the world he now understands it better than he ever did. It's a pleasure to recommend this spiritual gem." *Southern Cross*

ISBN 0-88344-1640 Cloth $4.95

IN SEARCH OF THE BEYOND

"*In Search of the Beyond*, the third of his works published in the United States, will confirm Carlo Carretto as a master of spiritual literature which lays the heart bare with the loving ruthlessness of St. John of the Cross, with whose mysticism and writing Carretto's works favorably compare." *Clergy Review*

ISBN 0-88344-2086 Cloth $5.95